Design for desktop publishing

John Miles

Design for desktop publishing

a guide to layout and typography on the personal computer

Gordon Fraser . London

Contents

7 **Introduction**

10 **Before you start**
Identifying the market - what is the document intended for and how is the reader going to use it ?

16 **Typefaces**
Typeface design - what makes the difference? Digitised type - high and low resolution. Type measurement - the point system. Type families.

24 **Typesetting**
Typewriter and typesetting. Good typesetting practice. Line length. Justified and unjustified setting.

28 **Page grids**
Page depth and margins. Column grids - with examples. Horizontal grids. Tabloid format.

40 **Symmetry and asymmetry**
Their influence on the layout. Asymmetry and space.

42 **Type and Layout**
An aid to finding your way about in the document. Main headings and subheadings - structures - spacing. Side headings.

47 **Emphasis**
Emphasising individual words. Emphasising passages of text.

50 **Indenting**
Paragraph indents. Indenting passages of text.

52 **Rules and boxes**
The use of rules and boxes in layout. Tint panels. Blobs and arrows. Initial letters.

56 **Quoted passages**
Quoted passages within the text. Displayed quotes.

58 **Preliminary pages**
Half-title - title - imprint- contents and other lists.

62 **Tabular setting**
How tables work. Type for tables. Column headings. Notes in tables.

66 **Notes**
Cross reference and footnotes. Annotations - marginal and cut-in notes. Small type for devotees.

First published in 1987 by
Gordon Fraser Gallery Ltd,
London and Bedford

Reprinted 1988

BRITISH LIBRARY CATALOGUING IN PUBLICATION DATA

Miles, John
Design for desktop publishing
1. Printing, Practical -
Layout -- Data processing
2. Microcomputers
I. Title
686.2'252 Z246

ISBN 0 86092 096 8
ISBN 0 86092 097 6

Text set by John Miles
Printed by
The Alden Press, Oxford
Bound by
Hunter & Foulis Ltd, Edinburgh

68 **Illustration**

Line and tone. Drawings - cartoons - charts and diagrams. Photographs - bleeding - cropping - positioning - captions.

74 **Cover design**

Basic principles. Standard covers. Tabloid mastheads.

77 **Colour**

Hue and tone. Colour and monochrome copiers. Colour for emphasis. Two colours without black.

78 **Binding**

Binding folded sheets. Single sheet methods. Some useful folds.

82 **Paper**

Characteristics of paper - finish - opacity - feel - weight - cost. Varieties of paper. Paper sizes.

85 **Reproduction in quantity**

Laser printer output. Copying machines. Offset printing. Preparing artwork.

86 **Planning ahead**

Making your own type specimens and line counters. Pencil layouts.

94 **Establishing standards**

Recording specifications. Style manuals. Correcting copy - printer's marks.

98 **Glossary**

102 **Further reading**

103 **Index**

Introduction

Design notes

These notes appear throughout the book to emphasise design features of individual pages.

Personal computers linked to laser printers can now produce a printed image comparable with, although not yet as good as, conventional printing. This has made it necessary for operators to make the sort of design decisions about layout and typography which have up to now been the preserve of the printer or the designer working within the graphics industry.

This book is concerned with the organisation of the text of printed documents which are produced every day by businesses, educational establishments, voluntary organisations and government departments. It contains advice rather than doctrine. It is not a manual of instant creativity nor is it an instruction book on how to operate a particular machine. Its purpose is to explain why print is better designed in one way rather than another and to help those who want to exploit the potential of the computer to produce documents that are more comprehensible, do their job better and are more pleasing to the eye.

Some personal computers are more sophisticated and have more facilities than others. It will not always be possible to carry out all the ideas offered in this book on every machine. It is the principles that are important rather than the individual manoeuvres.

It is always possible to supplement any mechanical limitation by hand. If, for instance, a particular program does not allow you to make up the pages in more than one column or get enough lines onto the page to fit your layout, you can always set the text in single columns - equivalent to the printer's galley proofs - and paste them up into any configuration you want.

Typographic design and layout are very agreeable activities. There is great pleasure to be had from bringing order out of disorder, from giving authority and style to a document that has up to then been just another anonymous typescript. But it is important to remember that it is only a means to an end: the imparting of a message from the printed page into an individual mind. Anything which gets in the way of that process is a mistake.

A few of the types of document that are likely to be produced on desktop publishing equipment.

The introduction is set in a larger type size than the rest of the text because it calls for a different pace and to discourage readers from skipping it.

Unless the designer and editor/author happen to be the same person there will always be room for disagreement about which is the best way to achieve a desired end graphically. A good deal of heartache can be avoided if the designer can establish at the outset the editorial limits of his or her role. Most editors will see the wisdom of cutting a few lines of copy to save a whole page. If it's somebody else's copy they will probably do it with some relish. If you want to make an editorial change to fit your design, it is wise to have a good reason for it - 'I like it that way' isn't really good enough, any more than the editor's response of 'I don't like it'.

Design and layout are at heart 'reasoned' activities but that fact should not inhibit the occasional flight of fancy which may annoy the purist but cheer up an otherwise dreary document. However, such typographical whims should be only *occasional* otherwise they get in the way of comprehension and irritate everyone. Just because the equipment offers a huge range of typographical possibilities from shadow effects to superscript there is no need to use them all at once. It is a matter of judicious selection based on experience, so good advice for the novice - if in doubt leave it out!

Before you start

The word processor is just as much a working tool as a chisel or a screw-driver. It may be more sophisticated but it will still only do as much as you make it do and the quality of its output depends on the skill of the person operating it.

Just as a joiner wouldn't go near his workbench until he had made up his mind whether he was making a table or a cakestand, so it is necessary to decide before you go near the keyboard what sort of document you are producing. What is its function and above all, how is the reader going to use it?

There will also be practical considerations. For instance ask yourself:

- Is it something that needs to be pocket size?
- Is it likely to be used by people with poor eyesight or in low lighting conditions?
- Is the information important but in fact only going to be referred to rarely as in the case of some legal documents?
- How many copies are needed? The more you print the lower the cost of each copy but a long run makes the cost of paper more significant.
- How is it going to be bound?
- Will it need frequent updating and will anyone bother to do so if you allow for the possibility?

The questions are usually much the same. It is the variety of the answers which drives the design and makes it necessary for one printed document to look different from another.

Some examples of desktop publishing.

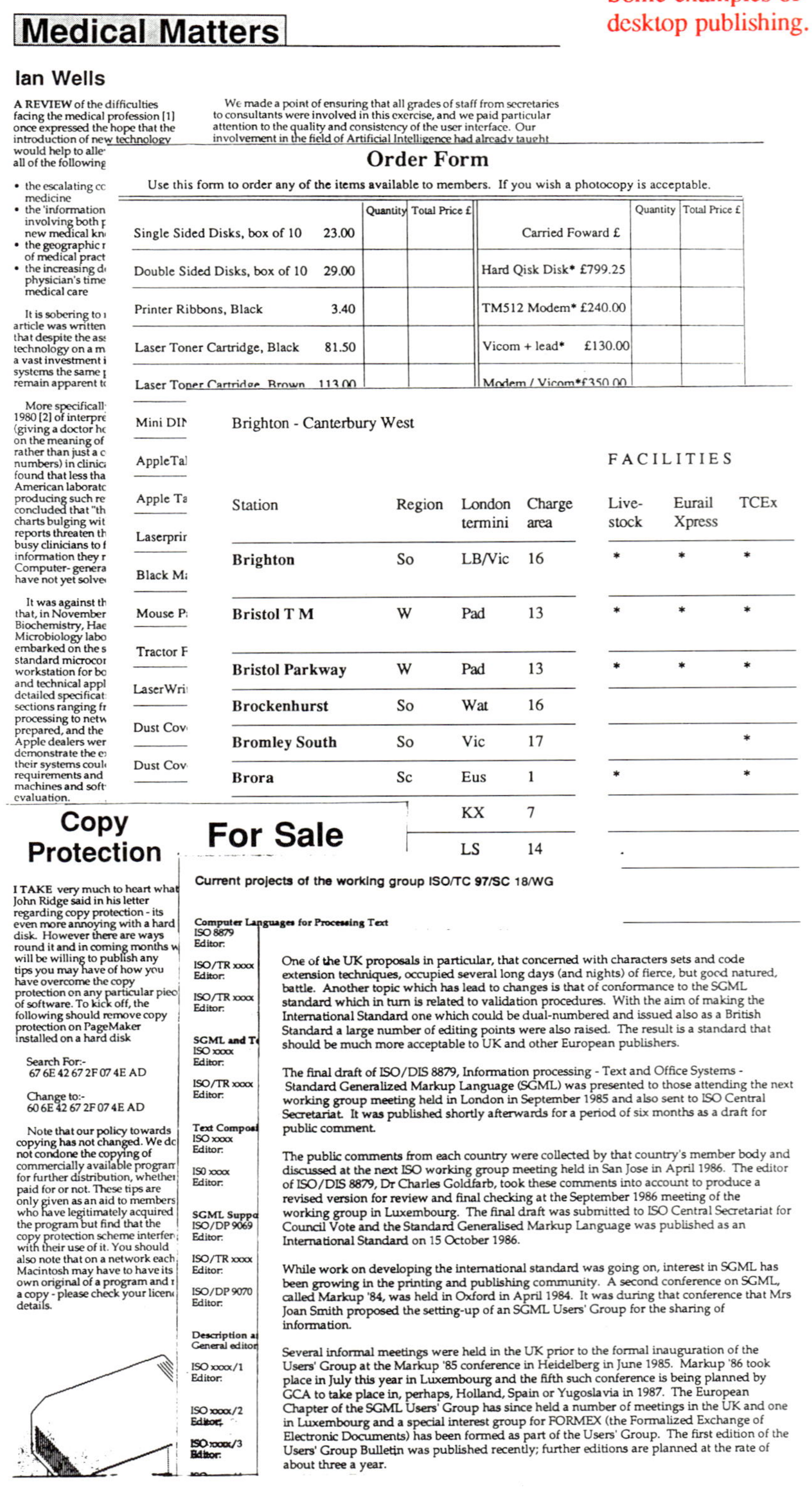
Medical Matters

Ian Wells

Order Form

Use this form to order any of the items available to members. If you wish a photocopy is acceptable.

		Quantity	Total Price £		Quantity	Total Price £
Single Sided Disks, box of 10	23.00			Carried Foward £		
Double Sided Disks, box of 10	29.00			Hard Qisk Disk* £799.25		
Printer Ribbons, Black	3.40			TM512 Modem* £240.00		
Laser Toner Cartridge, Black	81.50			Vicom + lead* £130.00		

Brighton - Canterbury West

FACILITIES

Station	Region	London termini	Charge area	Live-stock	Eurail Xpress	TCEx
Brighton	So	LB/Vic	16	*	*	*
Bristol T M	W	Pad	13	*	*	*
Bristol Parkway	W	Pad	13	*	*	*
Brockenhurst	So	Wat	16			
Bromley South	So	Vic	17			*
Brora	Sc	Eus	1	*		*
		KX	7			
		LS	14			

Copy Protection

For Sale

Current projects of the working group ISO/TC 97/SC 18/WG

One of the UK proposals in particular, that concerned with characters sets and code extension techniques, occupied several long days (and nights) of fierce, but good natured, battle. Another topic which has lead to changes is that of conformance to the SGML standard which in turn is related to validation procedures. With the aim of making the International Standard one which could be dual-numbered and issued also as a British Standard a large number of editing points were also raised. The result is a standard that should be much more acceptable to UK and other European publishers.

The final draft of ISO/DIS 8879, Information processing - Text and Office Systems - Standard Generalized Markup Language (SGML) was presented to those attending the next working group meeting held in London in September 1985 and also sent to ISO Central Secretariat. It was published shortly afterwards for a period of six months as a draft for public comment.

The public comments from each country were collected by that country's member body and discussed at the next ISO working group meeting held in San Jose in April 1986. The editor of ISO/DIS 8879, Dr Charles Goldfarb, took these comments into account to produce a revised version for review and final checking at the September 1986 meeting of the working group in Luxembourg. The final draft was submitted to ISO Central Secretariat for Council Vote and the Standard Generalised Markup Language was published as an International Standard on 15 October 1986.

While work on developing the international standard was going on, interest in SGML has been growing in the printing and publishing community. A second conference on SGML, called Markup '84, was held in Oxford in April 1984. It was during that conference that Mrs Joan Smith proposed the setting-up of an SGML Users' Group for the sharing of information.

Several informal meetings were held in the UK prior to the formal inauguration of the Users' Group at the Markup '85 conference in Heidelberg in June 1985. Markup '86 took place in July this year in Luxembourg and the fifth such conference is being planned by GCA to take place in, perhaps, Holland, Spain or Yugoslavia in 1987. The European Chapter of the SGML Users' Group has since held a number of meetings in the UK and one in Luxembourg and a special interest group for FORMEX (the Formalized Exchange of Electronic Documents) has been formed as part of the Users' Group. The first edition of the Users' Group Bulletin was published recently; further editions are planned at the rate of about three a year.

Identify the market

This is a general section so it can be treated differently from the more specific chapters later in the book. The cartoons help to emphasise the message of the text. They will be used more sparingly from now on.

ask yourself:

What is the document intended for? *and*

How is the reader going to use it?

The following pages give some of the possible answers.

To provide a simple link between the author and the reader in long prose passages.

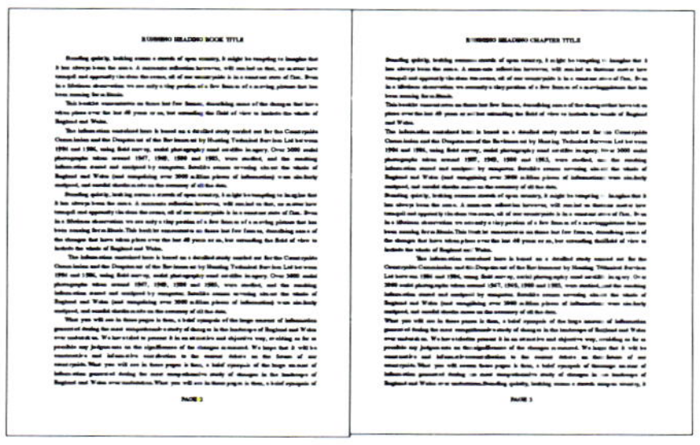

The reading will probably be sustained and in one place.

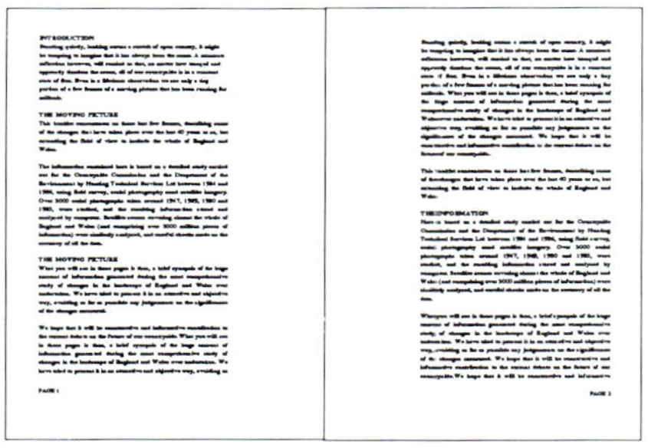

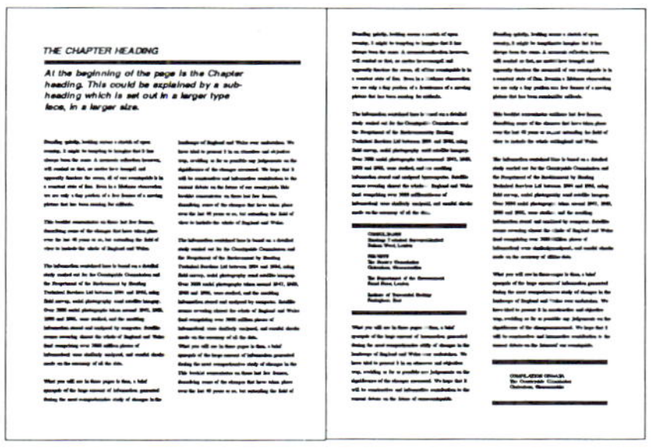

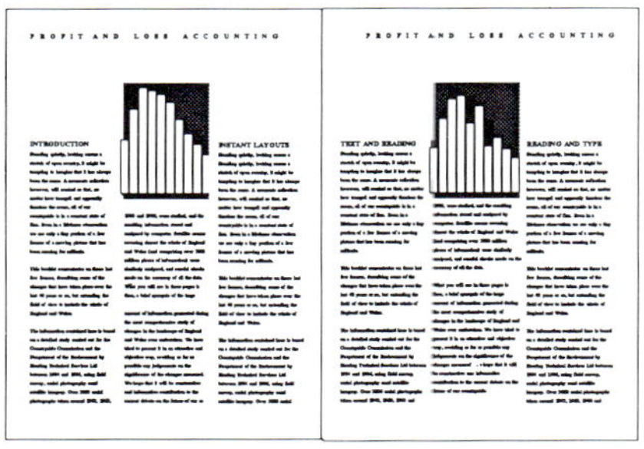

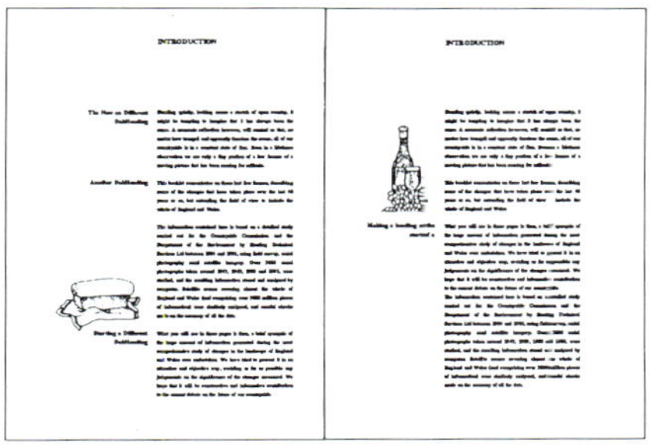

Examples

Fiction will probably be a leisurely read and if not compulsive almost certainly voluntary. The design therefore can be passive and congenial, not coming between the author and the reader. Everything depends on legibility and comfortable reading.

Non-fiction may also call for sustained reading but it may not be voluntary - it may be a chore with the reader's motivation much lower than for fiction. The very simple style suited to fiction may be a bit boring in these circumstances. Variations on the layout will help to make the text more digestible and give interest to the page.

Subheadings will break up the text into manageable pieces and act as signposts which help readers to find their way about.

The use of *more than one column* with the dynamic use of *space* and *margins*.

The introduction of *different type sizes*, possibly using *boxes* for information that is less important.

Illustrations can be used, particularly in the form of *charts* and *diagrams*.

Choice may have to be made between photographs and drawings. Photographs give an impression of reality but drawings allow particular points to be highlighted.

To provide information or entertainment in short digestible passages.

Probably read intermittently; sometimes on the move.

Examples

Newspapers, magazines and house journals are obvious examples. Much other information is acquired in this intermittent way. It allows the reader to assimilate information in relatively short pieces. At the same time it gives the editor/designer the opportunity to emphasise what he considers to be the most important facts.

The layout has to be more active. The shorter passages of text permit *narrow columns*. *Typefaces* can be varied. *Boxes, rules* and *tint panels* can all help. Don't overdo it, keep a balance between variety and confusion.

Again *illustration* is important, as is the use of *white space*. Space in layout is like rests in music. If everything is crowded one upon another you get a graphic cacophony.

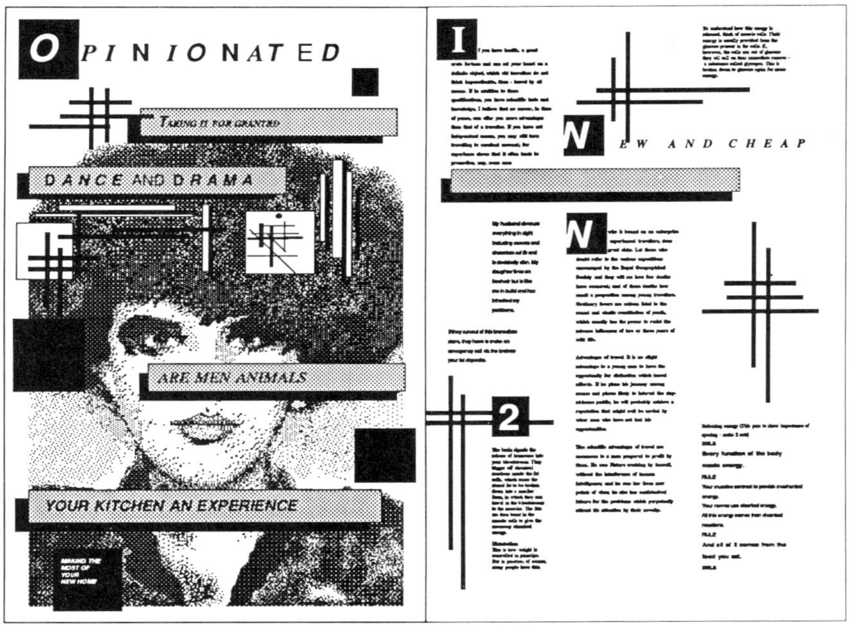

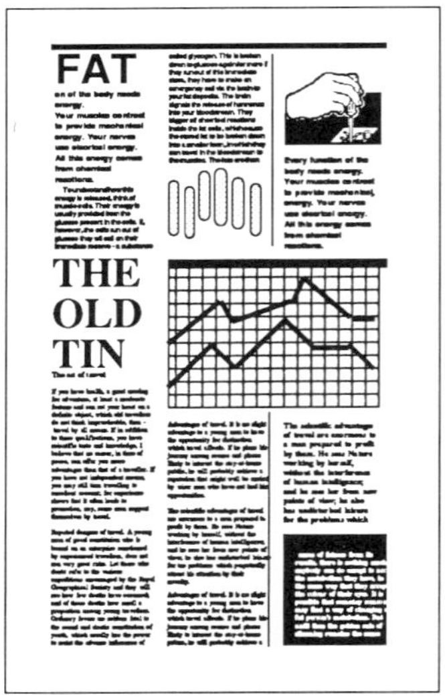

To provide reference material which the reader wants or needs.

Usually a short read after finding a reference.

Examples

Parts lists, dictionaries, encyclopedias and timetables.
In every case the reader is likely to be well motivated.

The first requirement is easy access to a key word or number usually followed by a short text or other information. Key words have to be emphasised - usually in *bold* - other devices such as *running heads* can be used to guide the reader.

Some documents in this group will have special problems such as *cross references* and *footnotes.*

The nature of the text too may demand a different *pace* for, say, an encyclopedia compared with a dictionary.

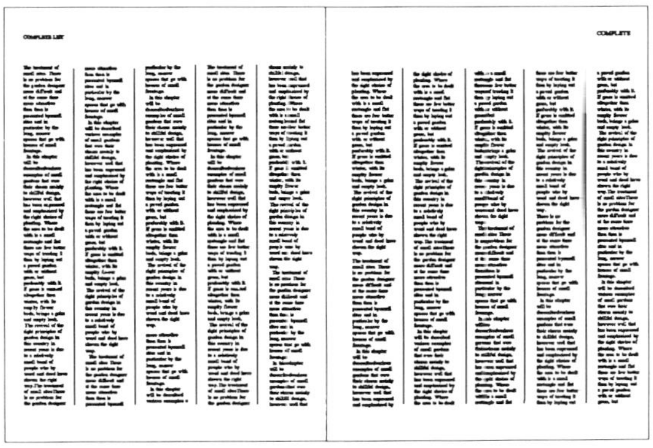

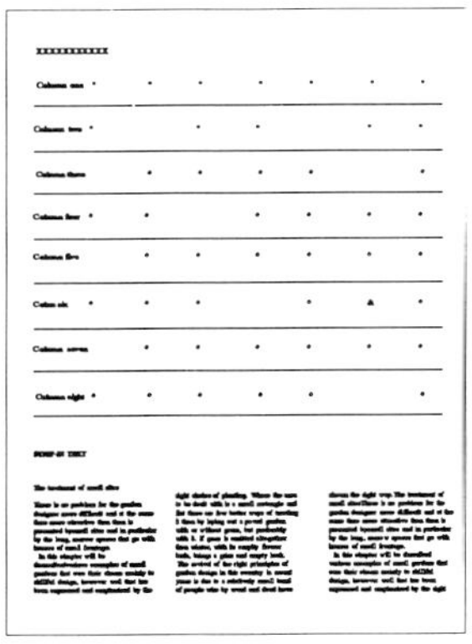

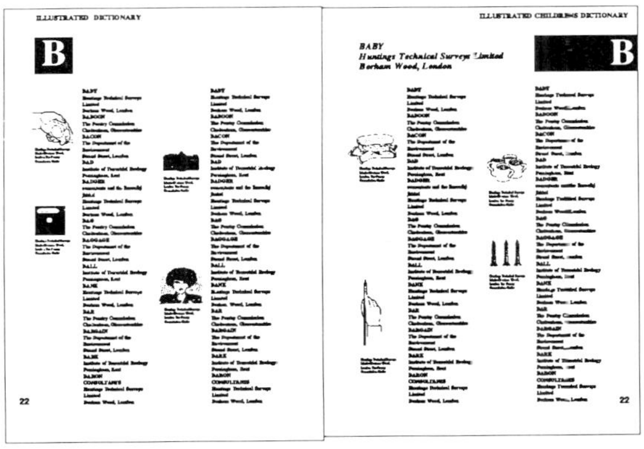

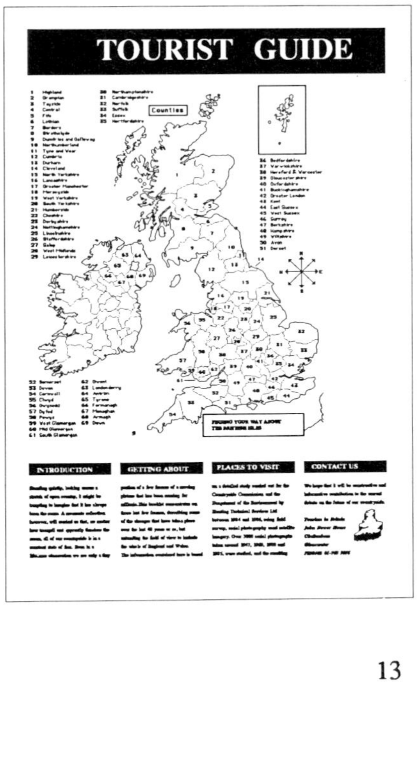

To impart information which the reader doesn't care if he has or not but which you want him to have.

May be read reluctantly or under compulsion.

Examples

A great many documents come into this category. If your potential readership has little motivation or even positive resistance you may have to call on specialist skills.

The *cover design* will be important. Readers will have to be persuaded to open it and then go on reading. Inside the document *emphasis* will be vital to get important points across. *Subheading hierarchies* should be simple. Useful devices will be *colour, arrows, blobs, rules* and *tint panels.*

For **mandatory signs** the message should be kept short, the layout clear, the style consistent and the presentation confident.

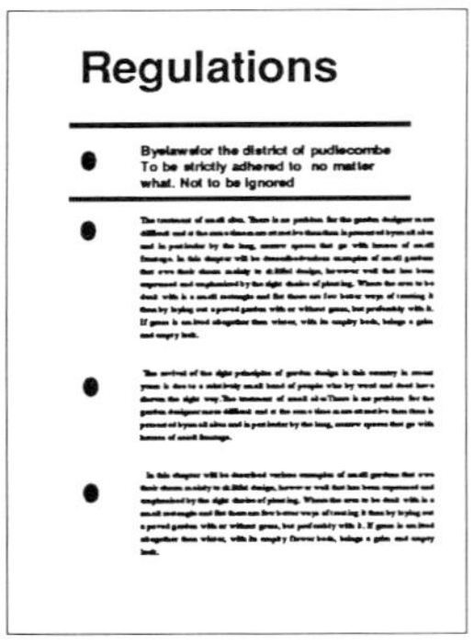

A guide to reader participation.

Following a step-by-step guide, possibly under pressure.

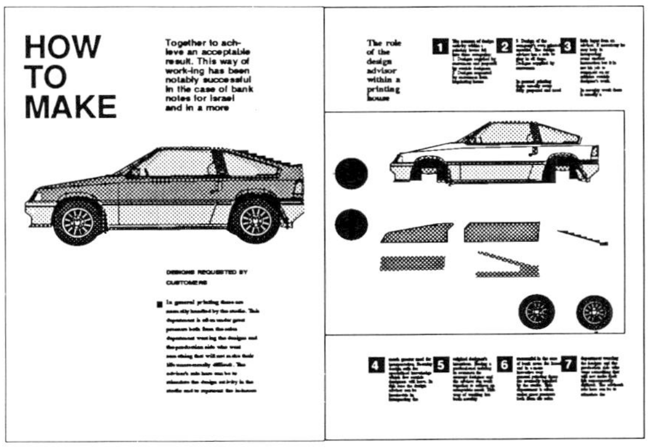

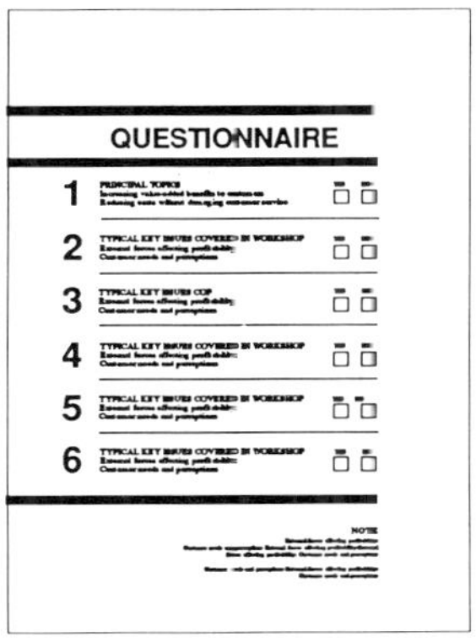

Examples

Instruction manuals, forms.
It will be important to separate 'instruction' from 'comment' by varying both the type and the layout. Like information will have to be grouped together or identified in some other way.

If a form needs filling in by hand leave enough space for each entry. A clear and simple layout to a form gives confidence to the person filling it in.

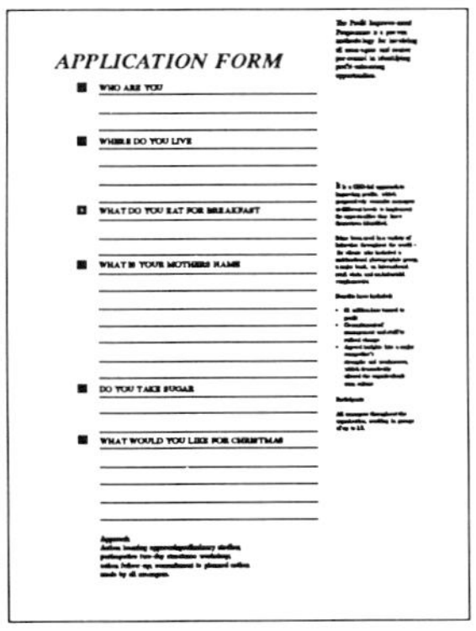

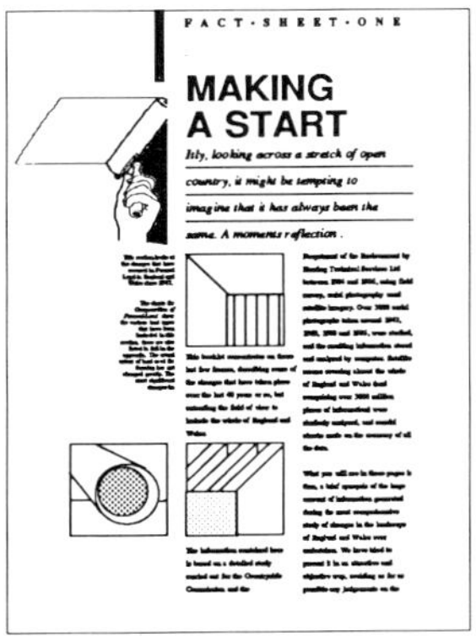

Most pieces of print can be fitted into one of these broad groups. Some will inevitably straddle uncomfortably over two or more. The important thing is to consider the function of the document before you start laying it out.

By identifying the likely readership and the way the document is going to be used you have established a basis on which to make rational decisions about size, type, layout and the other choices available to you, which are dealt with in the following chapters.

Typefaces

The style of a typeface can greatly affect the appearance of a document. The hundreds of typefaces available can make the choice seem very complicated. For most operators the choice is limited by what is available on their machine, but there are usually some decisions to be made. This chapter deals with the basic elements of typeface design which will influence those decisions.

Typeface design

Typeface design is an extremely skilled and subtle art. Very slight differences in a curve or weight of line can change the entire character of a letterform and profoundly affect its legibility.

Like other manufactured objects, letterforms have names for their dimensions and components.

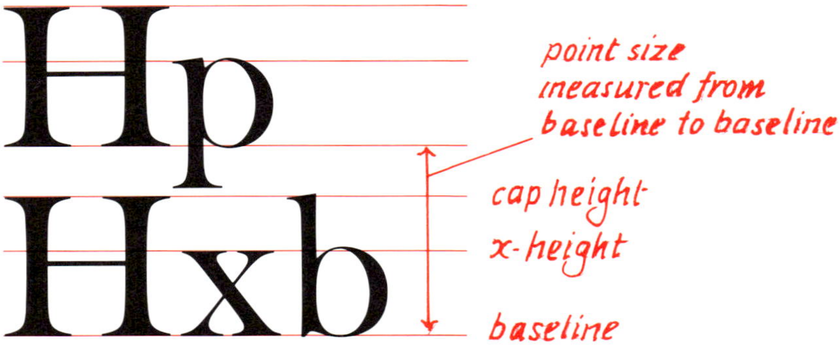

Capitals (upper case)

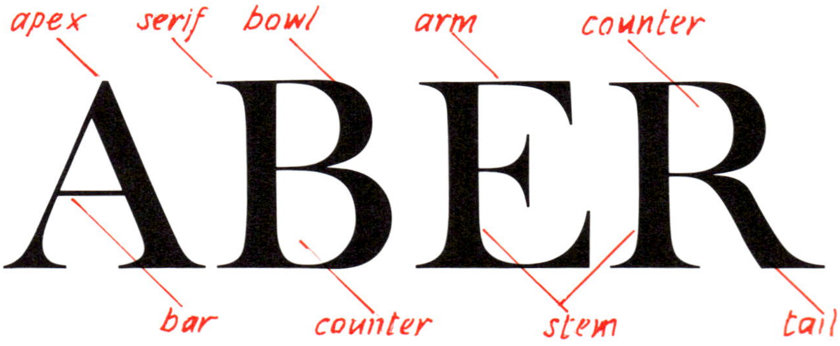

Lower case

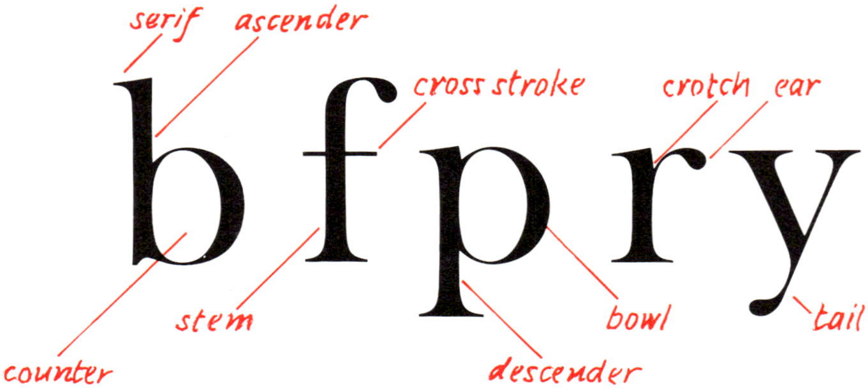

What makes the difference?
Many of the typefaces available may seem superficially similar but there are some basic distinctions which clearly differentiate one group of typefaces from another.

Printers and academic students of typography have for many years been trying to evolve systems for categorising typefaces, with more or less success. The problem is that very few types fit comfortably and completely into any one category but have characteristics which give them a partial place in another.

Very broadly there are four basic features which are fundamental to the character of a typeface.

1 Whether or not it has finishing strokes (serifs) at the end of the stems, arms and tails of the letters (serifed or sanserif).

2 The form of the serifs if it has them.

3 The amount of change from thick to thin in the strokes of the letter and the abruptness of that change.

4 The stress of the heavy part of the letter from vertical to oblique.

Apart from their technical differences typefaces have aesthetic qualities which can make them more or less congenial to individual readers and which can affect their legibility. Some typefaces seem more suited to one text rather than another. For instance a long legal document does not lend itself to a sans or slab serif type, while a directional sign is unlikely to be effective in a light-weight serifed face.

These are partially subjective judgements. My own view is that layout and the use of space is just as important to clarity and understanding as the use of a particular typeface.

H H

serifed sanserif

Varieties of serif

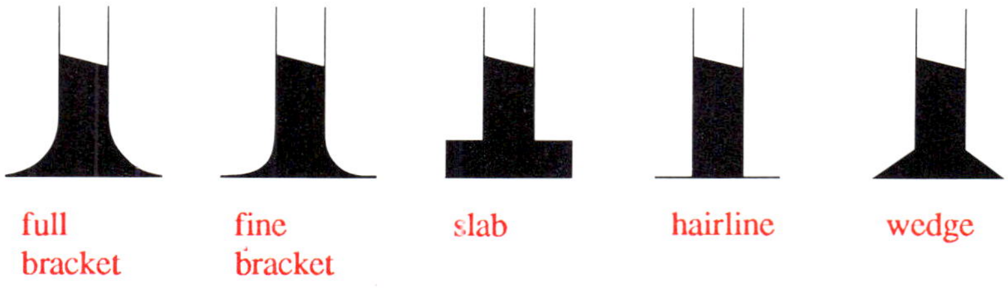

Rockwell: even weight - almost monoline, no obvious stress, slab serifs.

Honpe

Times: moderate difference between thick and thin strokes, oblique stress, bracket serifs.

Honpe

Modern No 20: Strong contrast between thick and thin strokes, vertical stress, hairline serifs.

Honpe

Digitised type

Laser printers and most of today's typesetting machines produce type in digital form. Each character is made up of very fine dots or 'pixels' which are stored in the computer memory. Because the dots are on a rectangular raster or grid, the curved and diagonal lines of the letters are made up of very fine steps.

Conventional typesetting machines use a raster of as many as 2000 lines to the inch (high resolution). This reproduces characters with great fidelity, particularly in large sizes. As the sizes get smaller the number of dots available is reduced and reproduction becomes correspondingly coarser (see diagram below).

There are variations on this basic digitising technique. Some methods use vertical lines only, others trace the outline of the letter by a series of straight-line 'vectors' before filling it in. For the personal computer user such differences in technique are largely academic. It is the quality of the image as judged by the human eye that is important.

Most laser printers use a grid of 200-300 lines to the inch (low resolution). So the laser printer output cannot be as sharp as that of the commercial typesetter. Nevertheless it can give a reasonable approximation of the original type design, particularly if the design has been modified to suit the resolution of a particular machine.

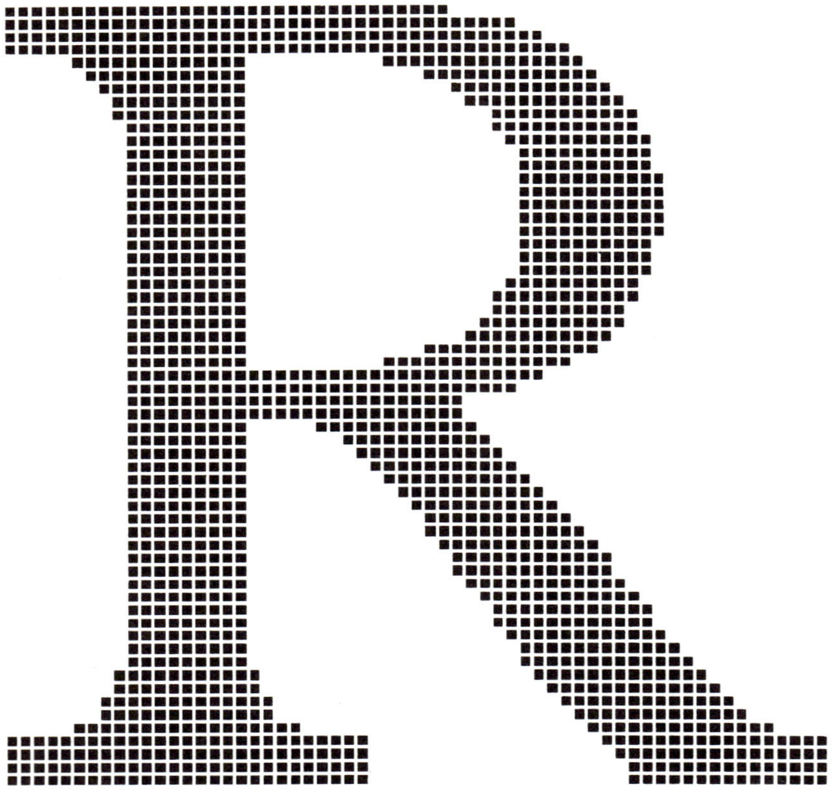

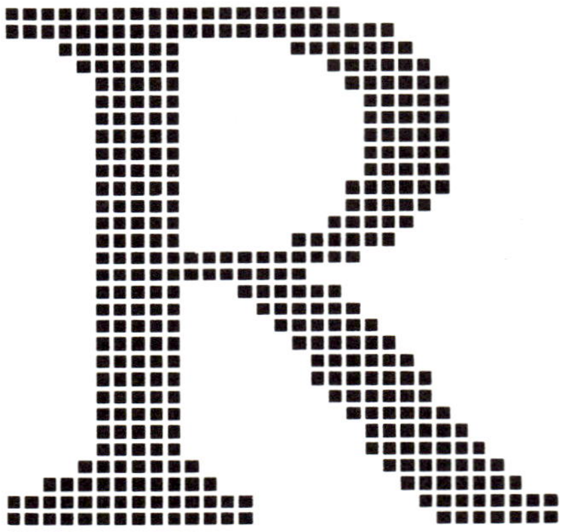

Simplified, diagrammatic representation of a digitised character.
The two sizes are both constructed to the same resolution. The bigger the size the more pixels are available to draw the shape so the definition can be more detailed.

The same text, set in Times, by a commercial typesetter using a machine with a high resolution compared with the output from a laser printer with a low resolution.

Besides the difference in the sharpness of the image there are some other interesting comparisons.

In the lighter weight, set in 10 point, the low resolution version takes up less width than the high resolution setting. This has nothing to do with the resolution but is because the characters are closer together - this is known as having a narrow 'set'. The set is in fact uncomfortably narrow and uneven. It is one reason why the conventional typesetting is easier to read.

The letterspacing of the line of capitals, while not perfect in the high resolution version, is capable of more subtle adjustment than in low resolution.

Notice also that the laser printer does not provide the 'fi' ligature in words like 'filling' and 'qualified'.

The bold version is set in 14 point which makes more pixels available for each character. The difference in quality between the two versions is less noticeable than in the smaller size.

Although both typefaces are called 'Times' their rendering is in fact very different. The low resolution version can only approximate to the real thing. However laser printers are improving all the time so by the time this book is published resolutions may already be higher.

high resolution

THE RECRUITMENT TEAM

low resolution

THE RECRUITMENT TEAM

high resolution

advertising and current remuneration levels not usually available to busy operational executives. As part of our role in relieving both the internal and external pressures inevitable in filling top jobs, we help our clients select from a shortlist of well-qualified candidates.

low resolution

advertising and current remuneration levels not usually available to busy operational executives. As part of our role in relieving both the internal and external pressures inevitable in filling top jobs, we help our clients select from a shortlist of well-qualified candidates.

high resolution

Most organisations find at times that they need to fill senior management vacancies by recruiting from outside. Indeed there are occasions when ‘bringing in new blood’ is strategically important.

low resolution

Most organisations find at times that they need to fill senior management vacancies by recruiting from outside. Indeed there are occasions when 'bringing in new blood' is strategically important.

Type measurement

Traditionally type sizes and all typographical specifications have been measured in 'points'. This is part of printing terminology which has been carried over into the technology of the personal computer. Originally the point size referred to the size of the type 'body'; that is the depth of the piece of type metal on which the 'face' of the type was fitted. So the size of the printed 'face' depends on its proportion on the 'body'. For example:

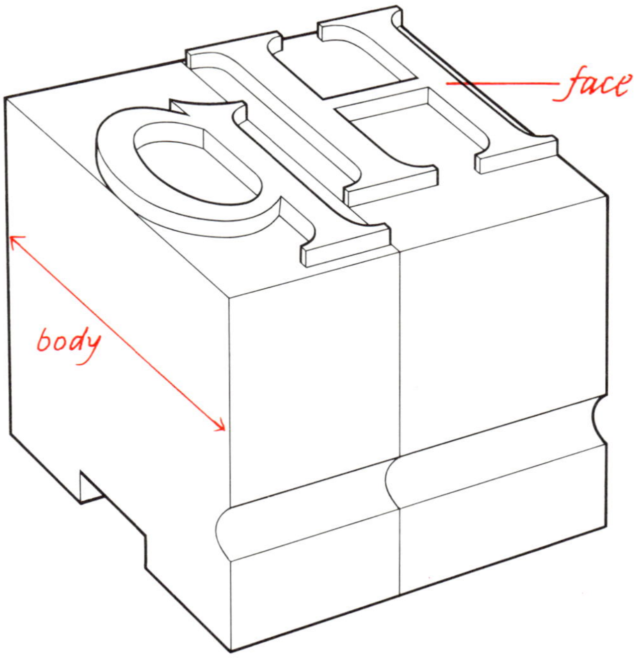

12 point Helvetica looks bigger than ...

12 point Times although they both occupy the same depth from line to line.

On personal computers typeface sizes relate approximately to the traditional type sizes but it is quite common for a 10 point type to be on the same body size as 12 point. This is not a serious problem providing that you are aware of it. Always run off a few lines of the type size you intend to use to see what you are going to get and what space it is going to take up.

The unit of typographical measurement used to specify column widths, margins etc can vary from one make of machine to another. It is usually in imperial (inches) or metric (mm). On some programmes both are available together with the point system. It is likely that, in time, all manufacturers will use the same system the most convenient of which, for Europeans, would be metric.

The imperial measurements are conveniently close to the British American point system. 1 pica (or 12 point em) is 0.166 of an inch (about 1 sixth) so 6 picas are only very slightly less than 1 inch. This is particularly useful to know when calculating margins if the paper sizes are given in inches and the typographic specifications are in points.

Unless you are preparing a specification for a printer it doesn't really matter which unit of measurement you use. I prefer the point system because I am used to it. Whatever system you decide to use, stick to it. When a number of workstations are being used in the same organisation everyone should use the same system.

If the program forces you to use an unfamiliar unit of measurement try to visualise and think in that system. Don't try to convert it in your head all the time to a more familiar unit. Although six picas is about an inch try to forget that and get used to the system in its own right.

imperial

metric

type scale in picas

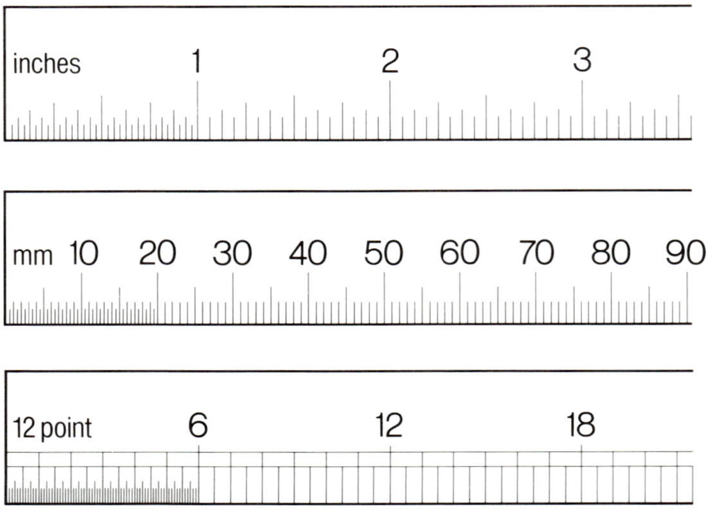

Interline space
The size of a typeface is defined by its body. If additional space is added between the lines that is usually referred to as 'leading' (after the strips of lead that printers used to space out the lines of type) or 'line feed'.

A type set on its own body size without additional line feed is said to be 'set solid'.

A 10 point type with 2 points of additional space between the lines is specified as '10 on 12pt'. A 12 point type with 3 points of extra space - '12 on 15pt' and so on. Printers will often refer to this as '2 (or 3) point leaded' or '2 (or 3) point line feed'.

Negative leading On some programs it is possible to reduce the leading to less than the body size. This may save space but the loss in legibility will be intolerable so don't do it.

10pt solid

The scientific advantages of travel are enormous to a man prepared to profit by them. He sees Nature working by herself, without the interference of human intelligence; and he sees her

12pt solid

The scientific advantages of travel are enormous to a man prepared to profit by them. He sees Nature working by herself, without the interference of human intelligence; and he sees

12 on 15pt

The scientific advantages of travel are enormous to a man prepared to profit by them. He sees Nature working by herself, without the interference of

negative

The scientific advantages of travel are enormous to a man prepared to profit by them. He sees Nature working by herself, without the interference of

The point system
There are two point systems in use in the printing industry: the British American point system and the Didot system. The Didot system is used almost exclusively in continental Europe. Personal computers approximate to the British American system. The units of measurement are:

the point, the en (half the square of the body size) and **the em** (the square of the body size).

the units of measurement used in personal computers are based on the 12 point body or pica em.

12 points = 1 pica (or em)

So a column 15 picas wide will contain 180 points. A column fifteen and a half picas wide is specified as 15 picas 6 points.

Checking the body size

To check the body size on a block of text - including the space between the lines - you will need a type scale divided into 12pt (pica) ems.

- Select a group of at least 13 unbroken lines.
- Lay 0 on the type scale against the base of the first line.
- Count the next 12 lines.
- The pica measurement at the base of line 12 will be the same as the body size (plus any leading) in points.

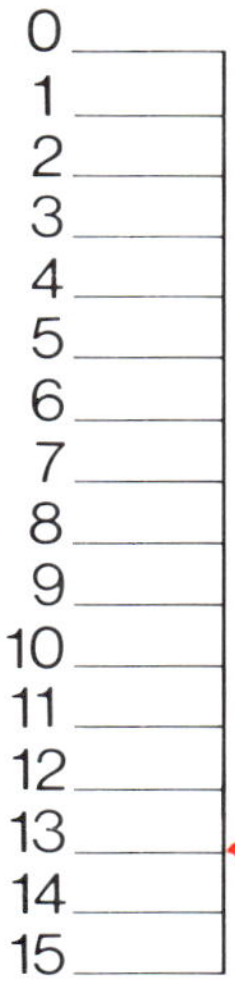

If you have health, a great craving for adventure, at least a moderate fortune and can set your heart on a definite object, which old travellers do not think impracticable, then - travel by all means. If in addition to these qualifications, you have scientific taste and knowledge, I believe that no career, in time of peace, can offer you more advantages than that of a traveller. If you have not independent means, you may still turn travelling to excellent account; for

end of scale on this line

this type is on a 13pt body

Type families

Most typefaces, both for text setting and display, have a family of weights and widths. These are usually derived from the original medium-weight design.

There are some types - particularly digitised versions of hot-metal designs - for which a family has not been developed beyond an italic, but the minimum expected of any new typeface today would be a medium and bold weight, both with italic.

A more complete family might include: light, medium, semi-bold, bold, and extra-bold, all with italic, together with narrow (condensed) and wide (extended) versions of all of them.

The advantage of these big ranges is that they can be married up and used together with the confidence that they will not only correspond exactly in proportion but that they will work together harmoniously on the same page. Few personal computers carry such big type families. The ingenious use of two weights is usually enough for most purposes.

In the four families illustrated here, the medium weight from which each family is derived, has been given a different title in each case (book, regular, roman, medium). The original weights are those most likely to be used for continuous text.

Examples of type families

Garamond	light
Garamond	book
Garamond	bold
Garamond	ultra
Garamond	light italic
Garamond	book italic
Garamond	bold italic
Garamond	ultra italic
Garamond	light condensed
Garamond	book condensed
Garamond	bold condensed
Garamond	ultra condensed
Garamond	light condensed italic
Garamond	book condensed italic
Garamond	bold condensed italic
Garamond	ultra condensed italic

The vertical rules help to hold together the very uneven columns, and make it clear which caption belongs to which typeface. Although the vertical grid has had to be changed to fit the illustration, the column of text on page 22 has not been forced out.

Helvetica	light
Helvetica	regular
Helvetica	medium
Helvetica	bold
Helvetica	light italic
Helvetica	regular italic
Helvetica	medium italic
Helvetica	light condensed
Helvetica	medium condensed
Helvetica	bold condensed
Helvetica	bold extra condensed
Helvetica	regular extended
Helvetica	bold extended

Plantin	light
Plantin	roman
Plantin	bold
Plantin	light italic
Plantin	italic
Plantin	bold italic
Plantin	bold condensed

Beton	light
Beton	medium
Beton	semi-bold
Beton	bold
Beton	extra bold
Beton	light condensed
Beton	medium condensed
Beton	semi-bold condensed
Beton	bold condensed

Typesetting

The principles of good typesetting are as important to satisfactory word processor output as to commercial printing. The techniques may change but the human eye does not and neither do the qualities that make for good, readable typesetting.

Typewriter and typesetting

The difference between typescript produced by a conventional typewriter and typesetting familiar in commercial print is easy to recognise.

On a typewriter all the characters take up the same width no matter how wide they look. This is known as 'fixed pitch' in which an 'i' occupies the same space as an 'm'. In order to do this the 'm' is artificially compressed and the 'i' is made as wide as possible with extra white space on either side. This makes for very uneven spacing between the characters which is one reason why typescript is more tiring to read than typesetting, where each character has its own width and the inter-character space is more consistent.

Legibility is affected as much by spacing as by letterform. Uneven or inappropriate spacing confuses the eye and makes reading slow and tiring.

Word processor output from an impact printer such as a daisywheel comes somewhere between the two but the effect is that of a fairly even typewriter. Laser printers however can come much nearer to conventional typesetting. This book has been set on a laser printer.

Typewritten characters all occupy the same space irrespective of their shape.

```
information
```

information

```
If you have health, a great craving for
adventure, at least a moderate fortune and
can set your heart on a definite object,
which old travellers do not think
impracticable, then - travel by all means.
If in addition to these qualifications,
you have scientific taste and knowledge,
I believe that no career, in time of
peace, can offer you more advantages than
```

If you have health, a great craving for adventure, at least a moderate fortune and can set your heart on a definite object, which old travellers do not think impracticable, then - travel by all means. If in addition to these qualifications, you have scientific taste and knowledge, I believe that no career, in time of peace, can offer you more advantages than that of a

Typewritten text compared with the same copy produced on a personal computer and printed on a laser printer.

The advantages of typesetting over typewriter are:

- greater legibility
- takes up less space
- usually offers a wider range of typefaces, weights and sizes
- adds authority to the document

Some people still find typewriting more 'personal' but this will change just as earlier attitudes to typewriter against handwriting have changed.

Good typesetting practice

We read characters grouped together in words, which are in turn assembled in lines. For clarity it is important that these groups be well defined. So the space between the characters should be *less* than that between the words and that between the lines *greater* than that between the words. Otherwise the words will run into one another or, if the interline space is too small, the eye will tend to drop down from one line to the next.

Word spaces should be as consistent as possible. It often helps, particularly when setting in short lines, to leave the right-hand side of the column ragged (unjustified) rather than force the line out to the right (justified). Justified type in too narrow a width can produce unsightly 'rivers' of white running down the column. To check for rivers, look at the page with your eyes half closed; the patches of white will jump out of the background.

It is not good practice to put space between characters to fill a line. It is not only ugly and changes the 'colour' of the text, it reduces legibility. Similarly the practice of double spacing after a full stop disrupts the even flow of the message.

Character, word and line space

When the space between words and characters is almost the same, the text is unreadable. The introduction of quite a small amount of space between the words improves clarity.

T h e a d v a n t a g e s o f t r a v e l. I t i s n o
s l i g h t a d v a n t a g e t o a y o u n g m a n
t o h a v e t h e o p p o r t u n i t y t o t r a v e l

T h e a d v a n t a g e s o f t r a v e l. I t i s
n o s l i g h t a d v a n t a g e t o a y o u n g
m a n t o h a v e t h e o p p o r t u n i t y t o
t r a v e l

When there is more space between the words than between the lines, reading becomes difficult. Extra space between the lines makes all the difference.

The scientific advantages of travel are enormous to a man prepared to profit by them. He sees Nature working by herself, without the interference of human intelligence; and he sees her from new points of view; he also has undisturbed leisure for the problems which

The scientific advantages of travel are enormous to a man prepared to profit by them. He sees Nature working by herself, without the interference of human intelligence; and he sees her from new points of view; he also has undisturbed leisure for the problems which

Modifications to the company's four high-volume cutback Sheridan binding lines, are being considered, but no decision on whether to proceed with the project is expected until the spring. The company claims to have spent between £1m and £1.5m a year over the last four years.

Last week Hazell had four Chinese visitors, staff from the Sino-British Printing Company. This is the joint venture in which BPCC bought a stake last July when Robert Gavron, St Ives

Rivers in a narrow column.

Cézanne, Paul
B. 1839 Aix-en-Provence, d. 1906 Aix-en-Provence. 1858–1860: studied law and worked at the school of drawing in Aix; 1861–1862: studied at the Académie Suisse in Paris, renewed a youthful friendship with Zola, met the Impressionists; 1862–1872: alternately in Paris and Aix-en-Provence; 1872–1874: with Camille Pissarro in Auvers-sur-Oise; 1874 and 1877: exhibited with the Impressionists; from 1881 mostly in Aix-en-Provence; from 1882 often in L'Estaque; 1895: first retrospective at Vollard in Paris.

More space between words than between lines, in spite of a reasonable line length and some hyphenation.

Widows
A 'widow' is a short line - the end of a paragraph - appearing at the top of a page. Until the introduction of mechanised page makeup this was considered very bad practice. Printers and typographers would go to great lengths to avoid them. Widows are, regrettably, accepted in even the most expensive publications today. They make a very uneven start to a page or column and it is still worth cutting a word or two to get rid of them.

Line length

For long passages of unbroken text, lines of about 60 - 65 characters will give the most comfortable reading length. In English this gives about 10 words to the line (each word space counts as one character). For shorter or more broken passages the eye can accept fewer characters, particularly if there is good interline spacing. Lines of much more than 65 characters can get very tiring to read but if circumstances demand such numbers some relief can be given by using a larger type size and increasing the space between the lines which helps to carry the eye along. The best solution is to reduce the line length either by increasing the margins or by using more than one column.

A comfortable length of line for sustained reading. For shorter passages, fewer characters to the line are acceptable.

If you have health, a great craving for adventure, at least a moderate fortune and can set your heart on a definite object, which old travellers do not think impracticable, then - travel by all means. If in addition to these qualifications, you have scientific taste and knowledge, I believe that no career, in time of peace, can offer you more advantages than that of a traveller. If you have not independent means, you may still turn travelling to excellent account; for experience shows that it often leads to promotion, nay, some men support themselves by travel.

Even when the line length is about right, legibility is greatly enhanced by extra leading.

Reputed dangers of travel. A young man of good constitution who is bound on an enterprise sanctioned by experienced travellers, does not run very great risks. Let those who doubt refer to the various expeditions encouraged by the Royal Geographical Society and they will see how few deaths have occurred; and of those deaths how small a proportion among young travellers. Ordinary fevers are seldom fatal to the sound and elastic constitution of youth, which usually has the power to resist the adverse influences of two or three years of wild life.

Alien objects are often applied not only to the metal plate, but also to the lithographic stone (Rauschenberg, Paolozzi, Clavé and others). Sometimes wood or plywood takes the place of the metal plate, and the surface is cut into so that during printing the paper is pressed through the holes, acquiring certain relief features (von Konow, Boudník and others.) Traditional size and regular shape have been abandoned, and the plate often displays irregular or 'ragged' edges, which add to its attraction. As a result of these techniques graphic art seems sometimes to be very close to sculpture and painting. For example where objects such as wire, scraps of metal and the like are applied to the plate, they create a relief which is so thick that in the printing process the paper becomes deformed or even torn, and the plate itself becomes no longer merely a design for printing but an *objet d'art* in its own right. It draws near to art where the artist uses a brush to 'paint' onto the plate a mixture of wood or metal shavings, fine sand

Too many characters - over 100 - to the line.
The word spacing is even and the leading is adequate but the eye still tires before it gets to the end of the line.

Ranging left

There is no evidence to suggest that unjustified (ranged left) setting is any more or less readable than justified (forced out left and right to give a straight edge on both sides of the column).

Apart from the practical considerations of word spacing in narrow columns, the choice of whether or not to justify is a matter of personal preference. My own is firmly for unjustified setting because it guarantees even word spacing throughout the text and gives a lightness to the page by making the most of the white space between the columns.

The only disadvantage is that if there are a lot of very long words in the text and there is no allowance for hyphenation then the unevenness of the right-hand side can be so extreme as to be distracting.

Justified setting can look very ponderous, particularly in double columns and, if the word space gets too wide and the operator finds hyphenation difficult, there is a temptation to space out individual words to fill the line.

The two columns on the right illustrate the difference between ranged left and justified setting. The justified text is too widely spaced. It would benefit from more space between the lines (leading) and some hyphenation.

Ranged left

If you have health, a great craving for adventure, at least a moderate fortune and can set your heart on a definite object, which old travellers do not think impracticable, then - travel by all means. If in addition to these qualifications, you have scientific taste and knowledge, I believe that no career, in time of peace, can offer you more advantages than that of a traveller. If you have not independent means, you may still turn travelling to excellent account; for experience shows that it often leads to promotion, nay, some men support themselves by travel.

Reputed dangers of travel. A young man of good constitution who is bound on an enterprise sanctioned by experienced travellers, does not run very great risks. Let those who doubt refer to the various expeditions encouraged by the Royal Geographical Society and they will see how few deaths have occurred; and of those deaths how small a proportion among young travellers. Ordinary fevers are seldom fatal to the sound and elastic constitution of youth, which usually has the power to resist the adverse influences of two or three years of wild life.

Advantages of travel. It is no slight advantage to a young man to have the opportunity for distinction which travel affords. If he plans his journey among scenes and places likely to interest the stay-at-home public, he will probably achieve a reputation that might well be envied by wiser men who have not had his opportunities.

The scientific advantages of travel are enormous to a man prepared to profit by them. He sees Nature working by herself, without the interference of human intelligence; and he sees her from new points of view; he also has undisturbed leisure for the problems which perpetually attract his

Justified (with paragraph indents)

If you have health, a great craving for adventure, at least a moderate fortune and can set your heart on a definite object, which old travellers do not think impracticable, then - travel by all means. If in addition to these qualifications, you have scientific taste and knowledge, I believe that no career, in time of peace, can offer you more advantages than that of a traveller. If you have not independent means, you may still turn travelling to excellent account; for experience shows that it often leads to promot-ion, nay, some men support themselves by travel.

Reputed dangers of travel. A young man of good constitution who is bound on an enterprise sanctioned by experienced travellers, does not run very great risks. Let those who doubt refer to the various expeditions encouraged by the Royal Geographical Society and they will see how few deaths have occurred; and of those deaths how small a proportion among young travellers. Ordinary fevers are seldom fatal to the sound and elastic constitution of youth, which usually has the power to resist the adverse influences of two or three years of wild life.

Advantages of travel. It is no slight advantage to a young man to have the opportunity for distinction which travel affords. If he plans his journey among scenes and places likely to interest the stay-at-home public, he will probably achieve a reputation that might well be envied by wiser men who have not had his opportunities.

The scientific advantages of travel are enormous to a man prepared to profit by them. He sees Nature working by herself, without the interference of human intelligence; and he sees her from new points of view; he also has undisturbed leisure for the problems which perpetually attract his

Page grids

The layout of the page is structured by the grid imposed by the vertical columns, the margins and the space between the horizontal lines.

Page depth

The page depth will depend on the size of type you want to use, the space between the lines and the margins. It will be easier to visualise this if you make a line counter (see *Planning ahead*).

The complexity of the grid will depend on the sort of layout you need. If the text is fairly straightforward and calling for a passive layout then the number of lines can be as many as you decide will fit comfortably on the page (or as many as the equipment will allow, which may not be the same thing) but if the layout is to be more complex then it is a great help if the number of lines is divisible by the number of horizontal grid panels you want to introduce.

Example
This book is based on a page depth of 62 lines of 12 point (most of the text is in 10 point on a 12 point body).

The page is divided horizontally into 7 panels of 8 lines each with 1 line space between each panel.
(7 x 8) + 6 = 62

Alternatively, by increasing the full page depth to 63 lines, with reduced margins top and bottom, I could have had 8 panels of 7 lines each with a line space between. (8 x 7) + 7 = 63

Having established the full page depth you can proceed to the selection of a vertical column grid. The column grid has to be seen in conjunction with the margins.

Margins

Classical book margins have their origins in early manuscripts in which the foot margin was about twice the head margin; the foredge was an average of the top and foot together, and the back was half the foredge.

Although these proportions are no longer adhered to, the general principle, modified to taste, still applies in book work. If the foot margin is the same or less than the head, the text will look as if it is falling off the page. The two back margins seen together will roughly equal the foredge.

Such margins are well suited to the novel or other continuous sustained reading but they do not permit the dynamic use of space and type usually demanded for more general publications.

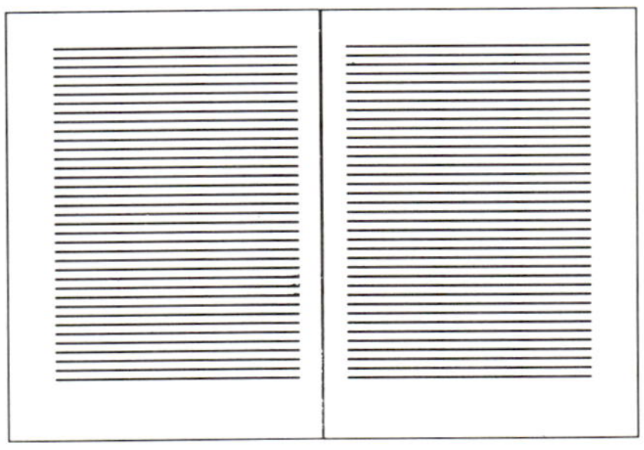

Classical book margins

When planning margins:

Always consider the layout in pairs of pages - a spread.

When considering back margins bear in mind how you are going to bind it (see *Binding*).

Remember to allow for page numbers and running heads if they are to go into the top and bottom margins.

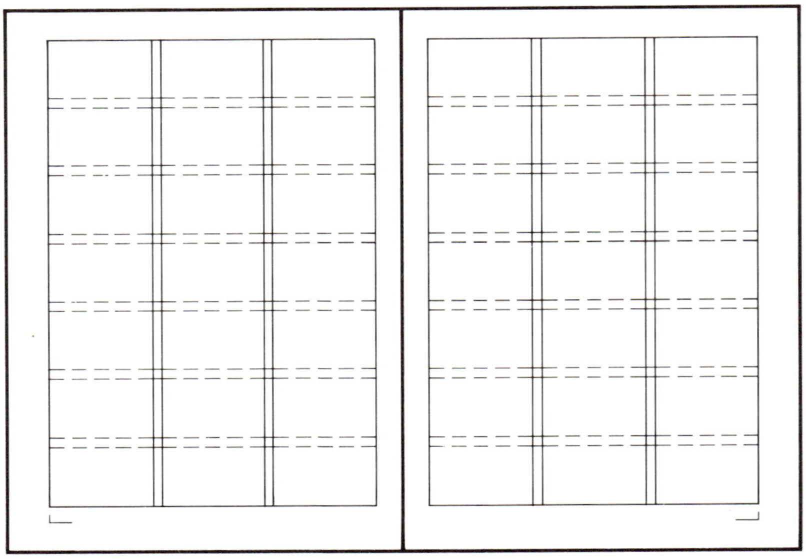

Column grids

The drop-shadow effect - which is easy to do on a PC - is reserved for the small illustrative example. The diagrams at the bottom of the page are left uncluttered.

Single column
full page width

Advantages Usually gets in plenty of unbroken text - economical.

Disadvantages The very long lines are likely to carry too many words for comfortable reading unless you use big type and extra interline space which is less economical.

The solid mass of text gives less opportunity to articulate subheads, secondary text and illustrations. The result may be dull and uninviting to the reader.

Most suited to continuous and sustained reading in a small page size , eg A5 (148 x 210 mm) rather than A4 (210 x 297 mm).

Examples of typical proportions
(all sizes in picas)

A4

text area
38 x 55

margins:
head 6
foot 9.5
back 4.75
foredge 7

A5

text area
26 x 39.5

margins:
head 3.75
foot 6.5
back 3.5
foredge 6

Single column with a big difference between the side margins

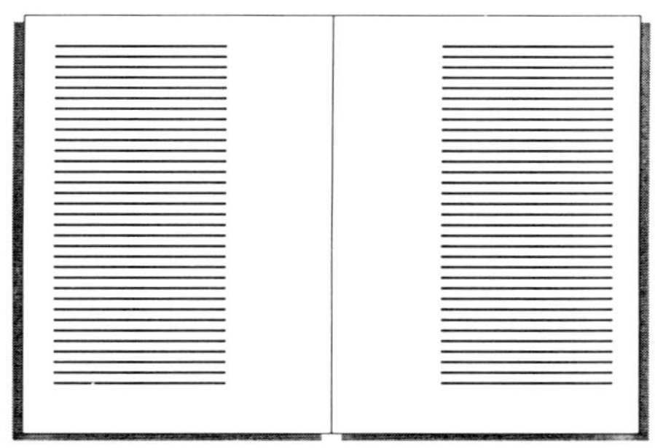

For the layout to be effective the column should be noticeably narrower than the whole page.

The choice here is between putting the extra space either all in the back margins in the centre of the spread or in the left-hand margin of each page.

If all the space is put into the back margins, the text on the other side of the page will fit exactly with the text on the front. This is known as 'backing up'; it has the advantage that it reduces unsightly show-through if the paper is not fully opaque.

If the margins are wide enough they can take small diagrams, illustrations or subsidiary text.

If you are expecting to use a ring binder or a method which makes it difficult for the document to open flat, the big back margins are an advantage.

If you insert all the space on the left of the text you can use it for side headings, subsidiary text or illustrations.

If you keep the proportions mathematically related then the left-hand side headings will back-up neatly with the right-hand edge of the text on the back.

Advantages Although not as economical of space as the full page width column, it still gets a substantial amount of text onto the page with the opportunity to introduce some interest into the heading structure. Makes for a more attractive layout for sustained reading in a large format document.

Disadvantage Still too static for an 'active' layout.

Most suited to sustained reading in a large format. Good for documents which have to look serious but benefit from some leavening.

Typical A4 proportions

all sizes in picas

text area
27 x 57.25

margins:
head 4.75
foot 8.25
back 16.5
foredge 6.5

Plenty of room for binding but not suitable for side-headings.

text area
25 x 57.25

margins:
head 4.75
foot 8.25
backs
left 4.75
right 18.25
foredges
left 20
right 6.5

Big side margins could take side-headings or small illustrations.

Ratio of column to side margin 2:1

text area
31 x 57.25

margins:
head 4.75
foot 8.25
backs
left 3.5
right 14.25
foredges
left 15.25
right 4.5

Smaller margin could take side-headings.

Ratio of column to side margin 3:1

Two columns of equal width

Advantages Easy to manage; usually giving a good width for comfortable reading. Can be more economical of space than a single column. The pages will back up well.

Disadvantage Can be dull unless skillfully handled.

Suited to almost any sort of publication. For this reason it is likely to be over-used.

Two-column layouts are by their nature static and so are less suitable for very active layouts.

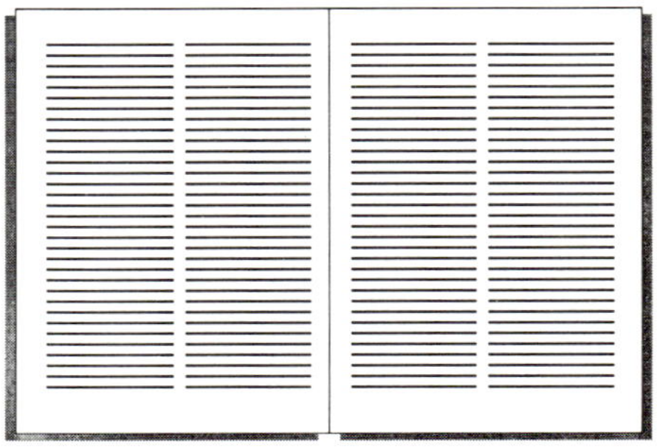

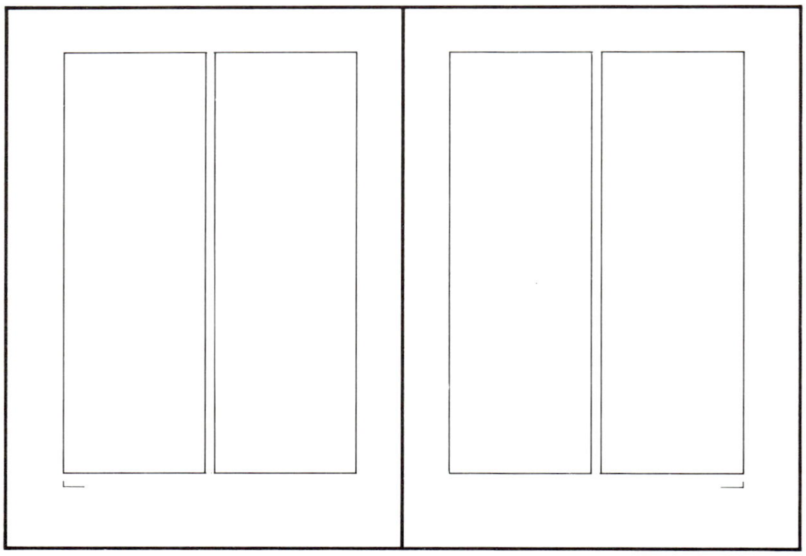

Typical A4 proportions

all sizes in picas

text area
2 cols of 18pica + 12pt gutter x 55

margins:
head 6
foot 9.5
back 5.75
foredge 7

Interest can be given to a two-column layout by using a big top margin to take the chapter titles and running heads.

text area
2 cols of 18 pica + 12pt gutter x 44.5

margins:
head 16.5
foot 9.5
back 6
foredge 7

Two columns of different widths

This only works if you have got two texts of different significance running in parallel, for instance a main text with a subsidiary commentary. Otherwise it is effectively the same as a narrow single column.

A useful proportion is for the narrower column to be half the size of the wider one allowing for the space between columns (see diagram) so if the subsidiary text unexpectedly runs out much longer than the main text, a page of two or three narrow columns can be inserted. Index and similar pages can be treated in the same way.

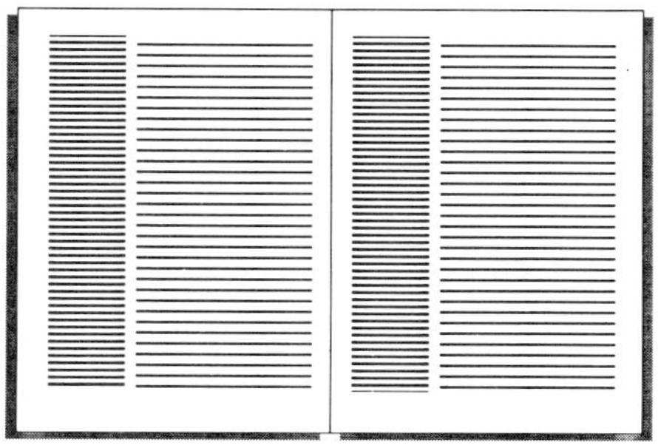

Typical A4 proportions

all sizes in picas

text areas
25 x 57 and
12 x 57

margins:
head 5
foot 8.5
back 5
foredge 7

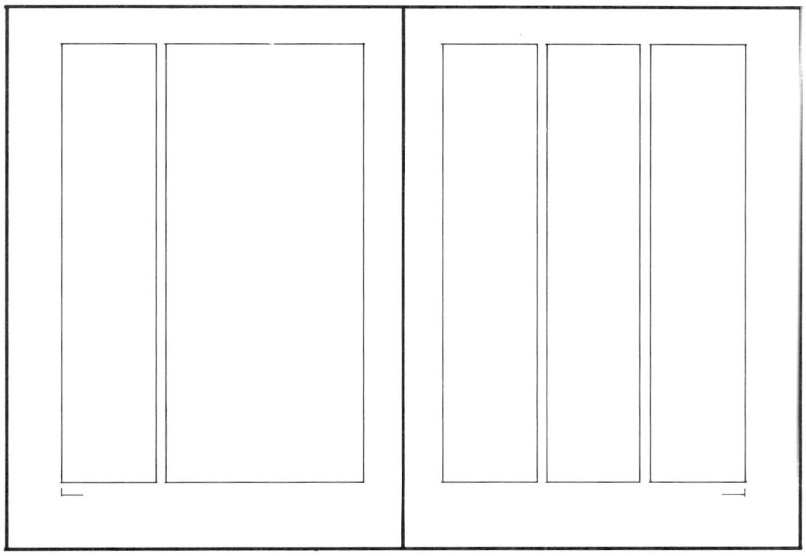

Three columns

Advantages A good grid for getting a lively, active layout. Economical but the narrow columns will probably dictate range left setting and the use of a smaller type size.

Disadvantage Unless the layout is well controlled it can become confused. It helps if you are willing to use a generous amount of white space.

Most suited to any document where text has to be combined with illustrations and diagrams or where the text has to be broken up with boxes and subsidiary matter.

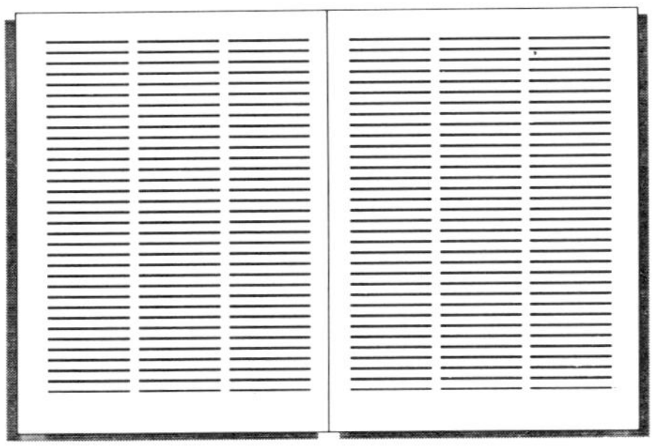

Typical A4 proportions

all sizes in picas

text area
3 cols of 13 pica +12pt gutters x 57

margins:
head 5
foot 8.5
back 4
foredge 5

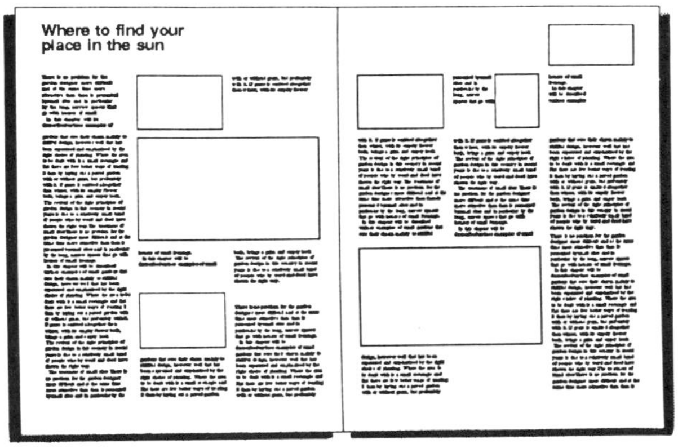

Four columns

Advantages Very economical for text with a lot of short lines such as an index or list. It can be the basis for a lively layout but the three-column grid can be easier to handle.

Disadvantages Relatively few characters to a line so the type size will have to be small and the text ranged left.

Most suited to indexes, dictionaries and other lists. Can be combined with a two-column arrangement for magazine and broadsheet layout.

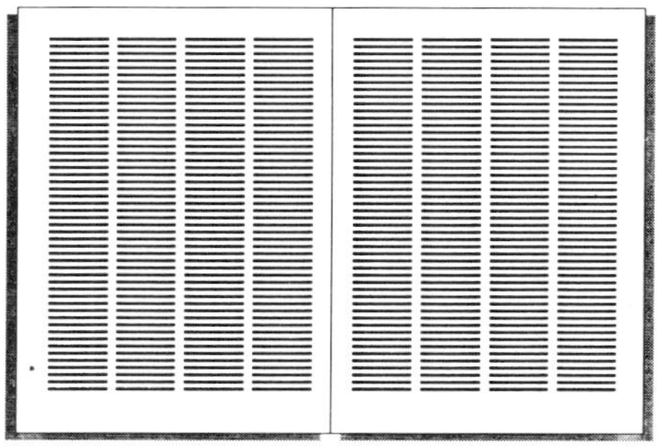

Typical A4 proportions

all sizes in picas

text area
4 cols of 10 pica + 12pt gutters x 57

margins:
head 5
foot 8.5
back 5
foredge 3.5

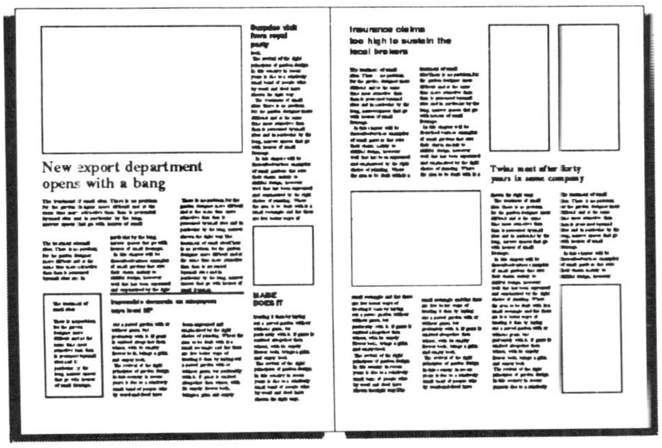

Horizontal grids

The advantage of a horizontal grid, used in combination with the vertical grid provided by the column widths, is that it imposes a discipline on what may otherwise appear to be a random and unrelated layout.

Horizontal grids are particularly valuable when illustrations have to be included, but their successful use needs experience. Too rigid adherence to a grid can create difficulties. If you try to force illustrations into a preordained space you may find yourself cropping or reducing pictures to fit the grid in a way that leaves them quite incomprehensible.

Most documents will call for some consistent, horizontal alignments. For instance, the opening text of chapters or sections should all start at the same height on the page.

A simple grid dividing the page equally into three or four parts can be a helpful guide in positioning illustrations. If possible the divisions should take up an exact number of text lines with a line space between each division, but if this isn't practical because the number of lines on the page will not divide equally, then simply divide the page arbitrarily.

If illustrations can be sized sensibly to come to the same height as the grid divisions this will not only look good but will make it easy to swap them round if you have to change their order.

The grid is there for your convenience and not to make your life difficult. A good designer will worry his way through the complexities of a strict grid layout and produce a stylish and elegant publication but it takes skill and experience. Don't let the horizontal grid dominate the layout. If you can't manage it, ignore it.

A two-column grid with very few and big divisions allows only a very simple structure. It is unlikely that all the illustrations will fit conveniently into a square or warrant the amount of space allotted to them by the grid.

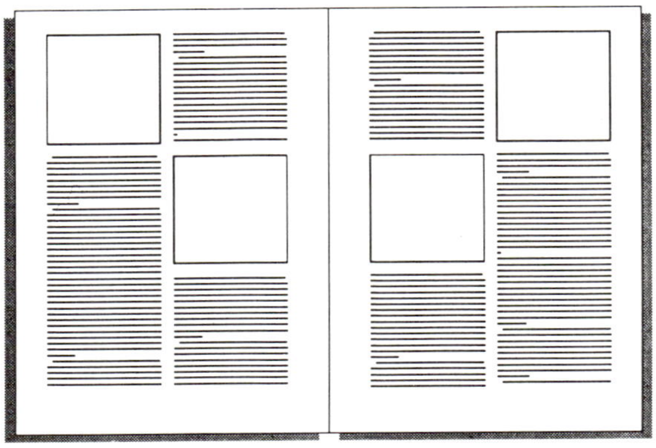

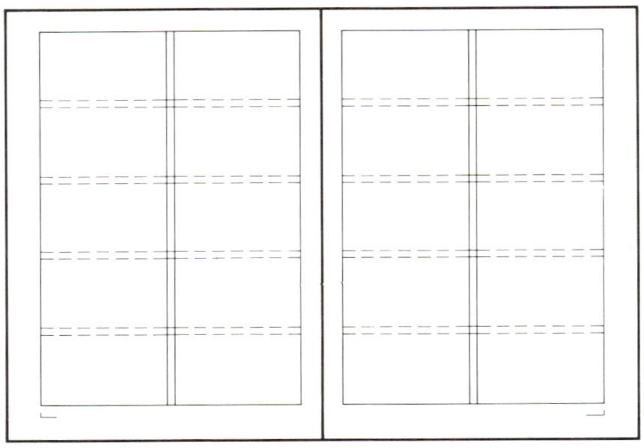

If the number of horizontal grid divisions is increased to five the layout becomes more flexible. The proportions given to the illustrations become more workable.

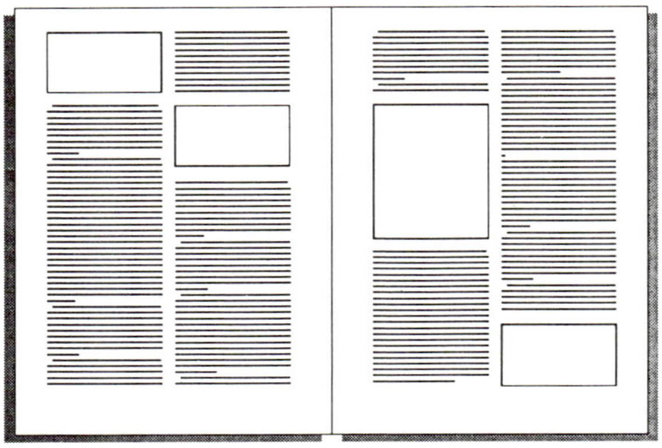

If the illustrations on this spread exactly fitted the grid of the rest of the book they would be too small. In fact they occupy one and a half horizontal grid units.

A three-column layout can take more horizontal divisions. The flexibility of the three columns and the number of grid units permits a lot more variation in the size and proportion of the illustrations. The discipline of a horizontal grid does not mean that the layout has to be dull and rigid.

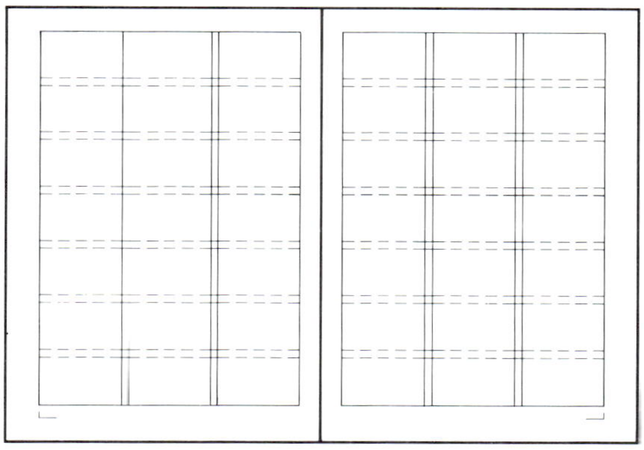

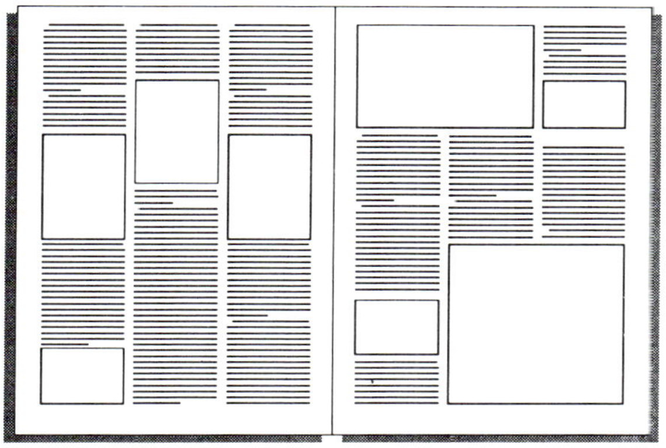

A four-column grid with eight horizontal divisions is particularly useful if a lot of illustrations have to be combined with text. Grids of this sort are invaluable in helping to control the use of white space.

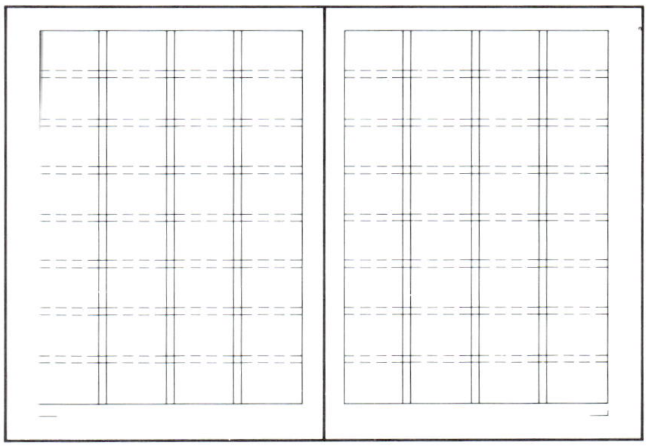

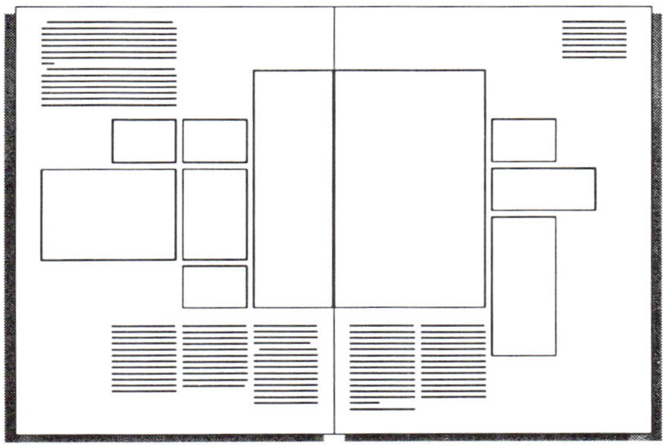

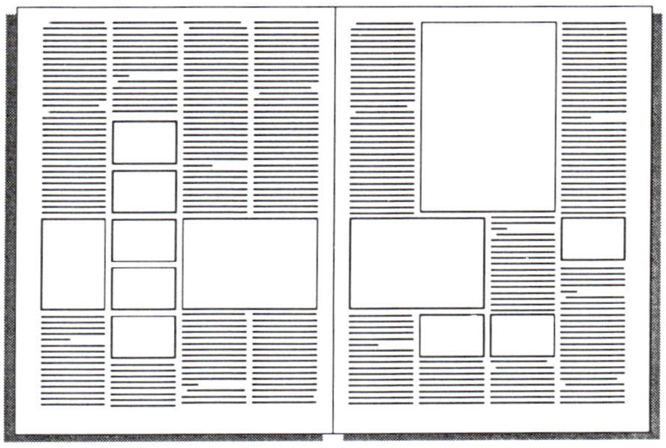

Tabloid format

Tabloid or 'broadsheet' is normally reserved for a document bigger than A4. The precise format may be dictated by the size of the printing machine but A3 (297 x 420mm) would be a typical size.

Both the format and the text suggest a newspaper layout. However hard many house journals try, they fail to achieve the vigour and immediacy which are among the attractive qualities of newspapers. This may be, in part, because the stories are not very newsworthy - even within the company - so that their styles fall uncomfortably between that of a magazine and a newspaper.

It is better to accept the text for what it is and produce a publication suited to the material and the readership rather than to contrive an imitation newspaper which lacks the 'news' needed to drive the design.

Columns
There will be room for five or six columns across the page. A layout using too many narrow columns will be difficult to handle and make for problems in word spacing. Too few columns, and it will be difficult to keep it lively. Text at the beginning of stories can run across two columns, in which case a bigger type size may be appropriate, particularly for the most important stories.

Above and below the fold
Broadsheets will invariably be folded in half so that copy will appear above or below the fold. Material above the fold makes up what is effectively the cover when folded. This is the obvious place for big headlines and pictures, but don't relegate only minor items to below the fold. Look at the page as a whole and leave some of the stronger items to appear lower down the page. Avoid having headings or small areas of picture on the fold.

Typical A3 proportions

all sizes in picas

text area
5 cols of 12 pica + 12pt gutters x 87

margins:
head 4
foot 8
back 3.5
foredge 3.5

Headlines
The layout will benefit from the use of contrasting weights of headline but don't use too many. The newspaperman's practice of having a list of numbered headline sizes is a good discipline.

Second (and third) deck headings need to be carefully chosen. Again, once a good style has been established, record it so that it can be called up again.

It will be a great help to the designer if he can sub-edit the headings to fit the space available or at least have access to an editor who appreciates the problem.

Rules
Rules and other devices can be important aids to directing the reader round the page. They can be used more widely than in more formal documents but not so freely as to cause confusion.

Typical A3 proportions

all sizes in picas

text area
6 cols of 10 pica + 12pt gutters x 87

margins:
head 4
foot 8
back 3
foredge 3

Symmetry and asymmetry

One of the most fundamental differences in a design is whether the layout is symmetric (centred) or asymmetric (off-centre).

The subject of centred and off-centred layout can provoke strong feelings among designers and design theorists who may object to one or the other in principle.

The choice between them profoundly affects the layout and feeling of a page.

In very simple terms, a symmetrical layout is likely to produce a more static, restful design while an asymmetric scheme permits a more lively and dynamic result. The question is not which is more desirable on doctrinal grounds but which is going to achieve the result you need to get a particular sort of information over to a particular readership.

Because a centred layout is so static it is very easy to make it pleasantly innocuous but boring. This is fine if you are publishing a novel with which the reader is going to relax quietly in an armchair, but it is extremely difficult to make such a layout arresting or to build into it the signposts a reader needs to help him through a complicated and demanding text. There is also a great temptation to 'balance' the page by putting illustrations in opposite corners. Of course some of the great typographic designs of history have been symmetrical but these have been achieved by highly skilled and experienced practitioners.

If you are building up your skills and gaining experience then you are more likely to achieve the result you want with an asymmetric layout.

In any case don't mix the two. Their effect is so strong that any attempt to combine them within the same document will look uncomfortable. If the layout of the text pages is asymmetric do not introduce a centred title page, use the asymmetric grid to produce a lively and attractive title page which sets the tone for what is to come.

Asymmetry and space
One of the great advantages of an asymmetric layout is that it allows for the more dynamic use of space. This is particularly important if illustrations are to be included.

How space is handled on a page will depend on the grid and how much space is available.

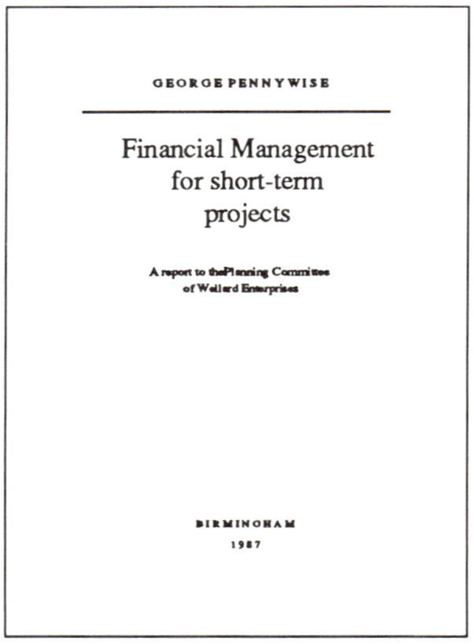

There are a few principles which apply to any layout.

- Do not be afraid of space or of using it dramatically. If a page has a white hole in it do not feel obliged to fill it up; use it to show the contents of the page to advantage.
- Not every column has to be filled with text. If the column runs short naturally, let it. Don't space the lines out to fill the page. This merely serves to change the 'colour' of the text and confuses the reader.
- Space is as much a graphic tool as bold type or rules and boxes. Think about it in the same way.

The same title page in centred and off-centre layouts. Each gives a different impression of the sort of document to be found inside.

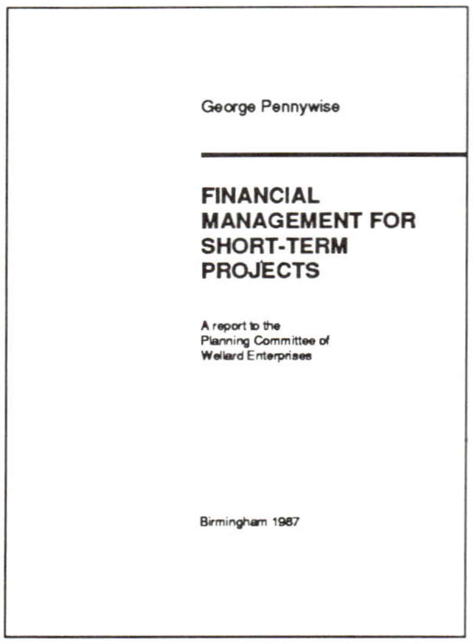

Symmetry sometimes leads to an attempt to 'balance' the page, which can be arbitrary and clumsy. Asymmetry allows more freedom.

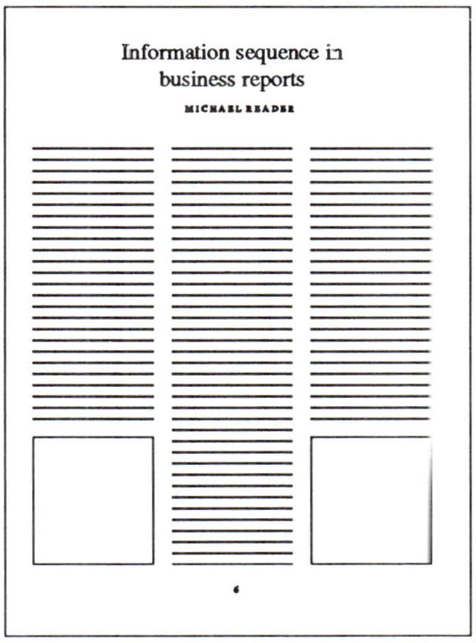

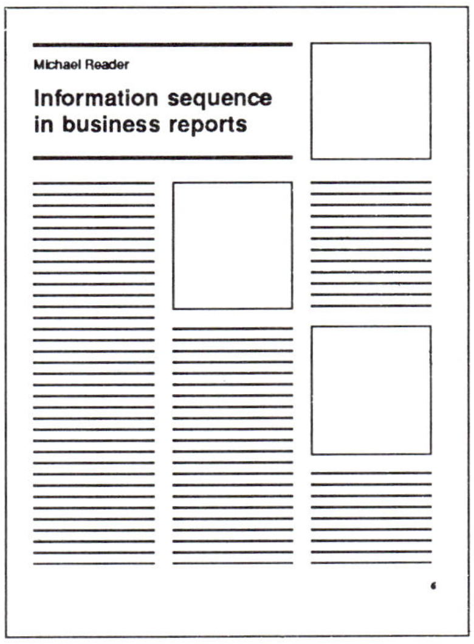

A clean, businesslike effect can be achieved more simply in an asymmetric layout.

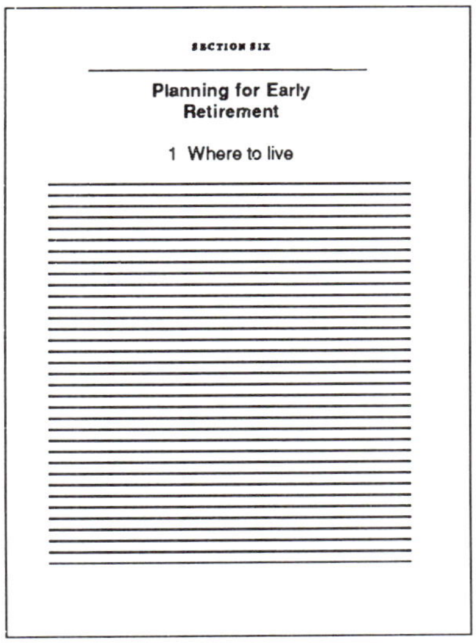

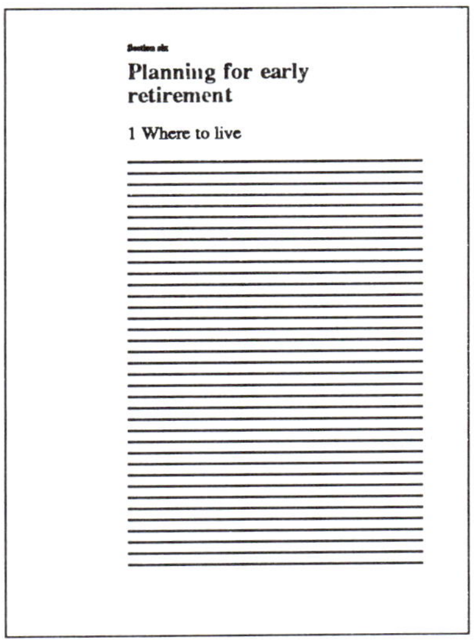

Mixing symmetry and asymmetry creates problems. Complicated material is easier to handle if you use one or the other.

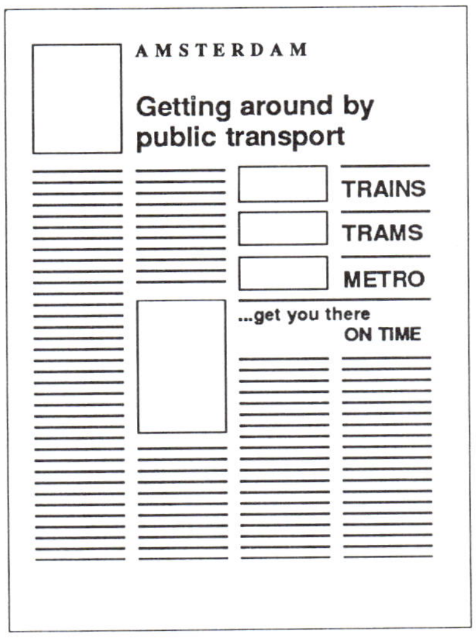

Type and layout

as an aid to finding your way about

Typography and layout, thoughtfully used, can provide signposts which reinforce the significance of each passage and help readers to find their way about in a document. Apart from arrows, blobs, paragraph numbering and other devices the most important element is the way in which heading systems are used.

Main headings and titles

The size and weight of a main heading or chapter title will depend on the range or hierarchy of subsequent headings it has to support. For instance in a novel the chapter title need be very little bigger than the text and still perform its function as a title. The designer may of course choose to make it much bigger but that is a matter of taste rather than function.

Capitals or upper and lower case

Whether or not you use capitals may depend on what is available to you but in any case always look at all the chapter titles before you start. They may be very different in length, in which case your choice will be influenced by the length of the majority.

A very long heading all in capitals may take up too much room or be difficult to read. If it's your own text or you have any influence with the editor, try to get the long ones cut. By the same token very short, single-word headings can look lost if they are not strong enough.

When using upper and lower case be consistent and sparing in the use of initial capitals. Use lower case only for short linking words such as 'the' 'a' 'to' 'of' 'which' etc.

If the text is divided by subheadings then the chapter title should be bigger and/or bolder than the strongest subheading. If the number of weights and sizes available is restricted, more power can be given to headings by the use of rules or background tints.

If the document is to be printed by offset lithography or run off on a copier, then typeset or dry-transfer headings can be stripped in, using typefaces not available on the personal computer. This takes time and trouble but if the document is important enough and with a fairly long run, then it is a course that can be considered.

The typographic treatment will be influenced by the length of the titles.

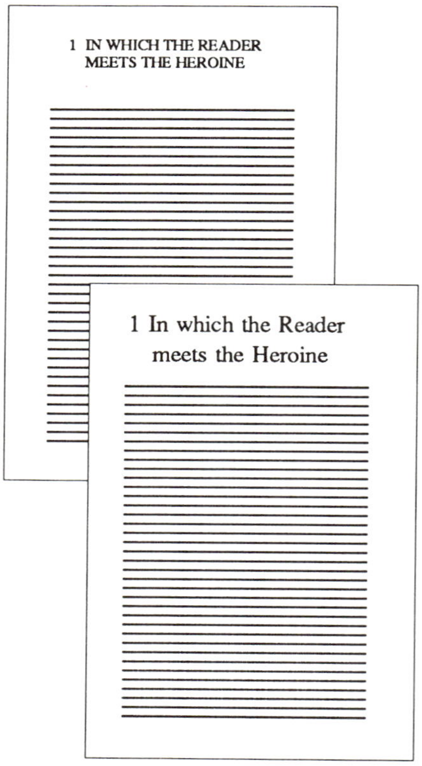

Five variations on the same chapter heading

There are, of course, many other ways of solving the same problem; including the use of rules, tints and initial letters. Although these may add weight and give emphasis they can distract from the message unless they are used carefully. Clear, simple typography is more use to the reader than overworked decoration.

Chapter 5

The treatment of small sites

There is no problem for the garden designer more difficult and at the same time more attractive than is presented by small sites and in particular by the long, narrow spaces that go with houses of small frontage.

In this chapter will be described various examples of small gardens that owe their charm mainly to skill-ful design, however well that has been expressed and emphasised by the right choice of planting. Where the area to be dealt with is a small rectangle and flat there are few better ways of treating it than by laying out a paved

One size larger in the same weight as the text can be enough for a title that doesn't have much competition from subheadings.

Chapter 5

The treatment of small sites

There is no problem for the garden designer more difficult and at the same time more attractive than is presented by small sites and in particular by the long, narrow spaces that go with houses of small frontage.

In this chapter will be described various examples of small gardens that owe their charm mainly to skill-ful design, however well that has been expressed and emphasised by the right choice of planting. Where the area to be dealt with is a small rectangle and

The same heading in bold naturally gives it more life.

5

THE TREATMENT OF SMALL SITES

There is no problem for the garden designer more difficult and at the same time more attractive than is presented by small sites and in particular by the long, narrow spaces that go with houses of small frontage.

In this chapter will be described various examples of small gardens that owe their charm mainly to skillful design, however well that has been expressed and emphasised by the

Centred capitals look more bookish, if that is what you want. Words like 'chapter' and 'section' can be left out.

5 The treatment of small sites

There is no problem for the garden designer more difficult and at the same time more attractive than is presented by small sites and in particular by the long, narrow spaces that go with houses of small frontage.

In this chapter will be described various examples of small gardens that owe their charm mainly to skill-ful design, however well that has been expressed and emphasised by the right choice of planting. Where the area to be dealt with is a small rectangle and flat there are few better ways of treating it than by laying out a paved garden with or without grass, but preferably with it. If grass is omitted altogether then winter, with its empty flower beds, brings a grim and empty look.

The revival of the right principles of garden design in this country in recent

A stronger opening can be achieved by putting the first paragraph in bold - if it makes sense - or by writing a special 'bold' introduction. In a two- or three-column layout the introduct-ion can be set a size larger than the text and spread across two columns, but don't let it get too wide. If the first paragraph is in the same size as the text it probably won't stand being stretched over a wider measure.

5 The treatment of small sites

There is no problem for the garden designer more difficult and at the same time more attractive than is presented by small sites and in particular by the long, narrow spaces that go with houses of small frontage.

In this chapter will be described various examples of small gardens that owe their charm mainly to skillful design, however well that has been expressed and emphasised by the right choice of planting. Where the area to be dealt with is a small rec-tangle and flat there are few better ways of treating it than by laying out a paved garden with or without grass, but preferably with it. If grass is omitted altogether then winter, with

Subheadings

Subheadings can perform two functions. They can serve to break up a long text and make it seem less forbidding and they can make clear the relationship of one piece of text to another.

Before selecting a subheading decide how many levels of subheading you need. Most documents can be managed with a maximum of three. Too many levels of heading with too subtle a difference between each will be lost on the reader and cause confusion.

for example if bold is available a reasonable choice would be:

MAIN HEADING

In bold capitals the same size as the text with a line space between the heading and the text. Avoid capitals if the main headings are consistently long.

Second level heads
In upper and lower case bold, in the same size as the text. Preceded by one line space but with no extra space between the heading and the text. Notice that in neither case is the first line indented after the head.

Third level heads in upper and lower case bold, the same size as the text, preceded by one line space and *run on* with the text.

---

alternatively the contrast between the headings and the text can be increased by changing the size.

MAIN HEADING

One size larger. This works well if the headings are well spaced out through the text. Try to get the heading and its space to occupy an exact number of lines of type.

Second level heads
Can be increased in size too but in this case they are getting too close in importance to the main heading so I would keep this level of heading to text size. *Run on* headings should be the same size as the text.

---

bear in mind...

Italics look different from but weaker than the surrounding text so should be used for very low level headings only.

If bold is not available try rules...

MAIN HEADING

Allow plenty of space round the heading. Let the rules come to the full column width no matter how short the heading. If some of the headings are very long and run to more than one line, rules will give those headings undue prominence because of the amount of space they occupy.

or you can improve legibility by letter spacing capitals...

M A I N H E A D I N G

...and increase the type size.

M A I N H E A D I N G

None of these three examples uses any graphic devices other than type. If other elements are introduced, such as rules, blobs or initial letters they are likely to look fussy and add to the production time.

The aims of National Parks

The preservation and enhancement of natural beauty

Although Parliament has used the term 'natural beauty' in defining the purpose of national parks, it has long been recognised that their scenic quality is partly the result of changes effected by human use over many generations.

THE 1949 ACT
The Act gave no responsibilities to the Commission or the park authorities in respect of farming or forestry. The scope for park authorities to influence these fundamental activities has been very limited.

Control of development The main power of the park authorities to preserve the natural beauty of the parks has been the planning and control of development under the Town and Country Planning Acts. One of the purposes of the national parks was to exclude unsuitable development.

Text: 10 on 12pt Times

Subheadings
A 12pt Times bold
B 10pt Times bold
C 10pt Times caps
D 10pt Times italic - run on

A simple subheading system; undramatic but clear to the reader. Few changes of size so not very time-consuming. Not very exciting either. Well suited to a text where subheadings appear frequently.

THE AIMS OF NATIONAL PARKS

The preservation and enhancement of natural beauty

Although Parliament has used the term 'natural beauty' in defining the purpose of national parks, it has long been recognised that their scenic quality is partly the result of changes effected by human use over many generations.

The 1949 Act
The Act gave no responsibilities to the Commission or the park authorities in respect of farming or forestry. The scope for park authorities to influence these fundamental activities has been very limited.

Control of development The main power of the park authorities to preserve the natural beauty of the parks has been the planning and control of development under the Town and Country Planning Acts. One of the purposes of the national parks was to exclude unsuitable development.

Text: 10 on 12pt Times

Subheadings
A 12pt Times bold caps
B 12pt Times bold
C 10pt Times bold
D 10pt Times bold - run on

More powerful than the first series but the difference between the subheading weights is not so clearly defined. Too many 'A' headings on a page would look clumsy.

The aims of National Parks

The preservation and enhancement of natural beauty

Although Parliament has used the term 'natural beauty' in defining the purpose of national parks, it has long been recognised that their scenic quality is partly the result of changes effected by human use over many generations.

The 1949 Act
The Act gave no responsibilities to the Commission or the park authorities in respect of farming or forestry. The scope for park authorities to influence these fundamental activities has been very limited.

Control of development The main power of the park authorities to preserve the natural beauty of the parks has been the planning and control of development under the Town and Country Planning Acts. One of the purposes of the national parks was to exclude unsuitable development.

Text: 10 on 12pt Times

Subheadings
A 12pt Helvetica bold
B 10pt Helvetica
C 9pt Helvetica bold
D 10pt Times italic - run on

Changing the typeface makes a clear distinction from the text. If a different typeface is to be used it should be clearly different (eg serif against sanserif) otherwise it will look like a mistake.The heading structure will be clear to the reader but if headings appear frequently, changing the typeface and weights will take up a lot of time.

Spacing subheadings

The amount of space round a subhead should reflect its importance in the hierarchy.

The heading should be closer to the text it refers to than to the preceding text.

So if, as in the example below, the main heading is preceded by a two-line space and followed by a one-line space...

F I R S T S U B H E A D

Then the next level of heading might have single line space above and below.

Second subhead

While the third level would have only one line of space above it and no extra space below.

Third subhead
This principle of spacing subheadings applies also to headings with rules or background tints.

Unlike commercial typesetters, most personal computers limit spaces to units of a whole line. Although this reduces the opportunity for very subtle increments in spacing, it does mean that all full columns will come to the same length and the pages can back up well.

The line immediately following a subheading should be set flush to the left. Sometimes, particularly in newspapers and magazines, an indent appears after a subheading. This is because the subheadings are inserted at the beginning of a paragraph after the text has been set and the paragraph indent has not been removed. This would have been slow and costly in the days of metal type but the word processor keyboard presents no such problems.

A heading system not thought through

The initial letter seems to work on one page...

residual voltage is required, a high-power foldback diode has been developed.

5. Protection issues in the future

The experience gained in protecting exchange interfaces will be invaluable when designing the sophisticated systems which will be used to provide future tele-

....

...but is inappropriate on another. The variations in indent add to the confusion.

V, again excluding low-power stations (below 10 kW ERP).

5. Engineering studies related to television signal and transmission standards, and testing methods

5.1 Television transmission standards

By 1937, with the decision of the Television Committee in favour of the Marconi-EMI system as opposed to the Baird system, the 405-line monochrome television signal standard using the waveform developed by A D Blumlein et al was virtually established in all its essential details [16].

5.2 Television transmission standards

However, much remained to be done to establish satisfactory transmission standards, e.g. with regard to:

- signal-to-random noise, single-frequency and pulse interference ratios,

Side headings

If you are using a wide column of text with a generous side margin then there may be room to use side headings.

Side headings Side headings serve to index the text rather than break it up. You can read through the text and ignore side headings, whereas a heading within the columns makes a more obvious break.

Keeping pace with the relevant text Because side headings have to keep pace with the text to which they refer they are best kept to the same size as the bulk of the text. Otherwise if the heading runs to more than one line it will start to get out of step. It also keeps keyboarding simple.

Side headings and text with very short paragraphs Make sure that there are not many short paragraphs each with its own heading.

Next subheading If the heading in the narrow column runs to more lines than the text in the wide column it makes ugly and confusing gaps.

Emphasis

Emphasis is defined by the Oxford Dictionary as 'Stress laid on word(s) to indicate special significance'. The choice of what is significant is an editorial rather than a design decision but it is important to remember that if **emphasis** is sprayed about indiscriminately then nothing will seem important.

Emphasising individual words

Bold is the easiest and most effective means of giving emphasis but it may confuse with or limit the variety of bold subheadings.

The **elk of Northern Europe and Asia** and the **moose of North America** are very similar in both habit and appearance; in fact they are so closely connected that some scientists regard them as the same species They are the largest members of the deer family and are distinguished by their long legs, short neck and broad muzzle. The antlers, which are generally broadly palmated grow from the side of the forehead at right angles to the skull. The antlers of the **moose** greatly exceed those of the **elk** in spread.

Italic will change the pace sufficiently and be less insistent than bold but it may already be designated for foreign or scientific words.

The *elk of Northern Europe and Asia* and the *moose of North America* are very similar in both habit and appearance; in fact they are so closely connected that some scientists regard them as the same species. They are the largest members of the deer family and are distinguished by their long legs, short neck and broad muzzle. The antlers, which are generally broadly palmated grow from the side of the forehead at right angles to the skull. The antlers of the *moose* greatly exceed those of the *elk* in spread.

CAPITALS (ROMAN, **BOLD** or *ITALIC*) give very strong emphasis so they should be used only if a few individual words need emphasis.

The ELK OF NORTHERN EUROPE AND ASIA and the MOOSE OF NORTH AMERICA are very similar in both habit and appearance; in fact they are so closely connected that some scientists regard them as the same species. They are the largest members of the deer family and are distinguished by their long legs, short neck and broad muzzle. The antlers, which are generally broadly palmated grow from the side of the forehead at right angles to the skull. The antlers of the MOOSE greatly exceed those of the ELK in spread.

Underlining is a clumsy hangover from the typewriter and should be used only if nothing better is available. It can also cause confusion in copy preparation as underlining is the conventional sign that a word should be printed in italic.

The elk of Northern Europe and Asia and the moose of North America are very similar in both habit and appearance; in fact they are so closely connected that some scientists regard them as the same species. They are the largest members of the deer family and are distinguished by their long legs, short neck and broad muzzle. The antlers, which are generally broadly palmated grow from the side of the forehead at right angles to the skull. The antlers of the moose greatly exceed those of the elk in spread.

L e t t e r s p a c i n g is not very effective. It makes for a very uneven page and breaks the flow of the text.

The e l k o f N o r t h e r n E u r o p e and the m o o s e o f N o r t h A m e r i c a are very similar in both habit and appearance; in fact they are so closely connected that some scientists regard them as the same species. They are the largest members of the deer family and are distinguished by their long legs, short neck and broad muzzle. The antlers, which are generally broadly palmated grow from the side of the forehead at right angles to the skull. The antlers of a m o o s e greatly exceed those of an e l k in spread.

Whatever device is used, it must be carried through consistently otherwise the reader will be confused.

Emphasising sentences and paragraphs

Complete sentences or paragraphs can be set all in bold or italic to give them emphasis.This can be a useful technique when you want to gain the readers' interest by emphasising salient points, in the expectation that that is all they will have time for.

Although italic changes the pace of the text and so catches the eye, it is for the most part weaker and less legible than bold.

If the emphasised passages are well spread out they could be in a size larger than the surrounding text but do not do this if they are too close to one another or the effect will be confusing.

The same end can be achieved by spacing or indenting (see *Quoted passages*).

It is sometimes helpful to emphasise the opening paragraph to a particular passage, for instance at the beginning of a chapter.

Space can be as important in giving emphasis as size and weight. The typefaces used in both these examples are exactly the same but, even in a reduced scale, it is clear that the one on the right gains by having more space through the emphasised paragraphs.

Every function of the body needs energy.
Your muscles contract to provide mechanical energy.
Your nerves use electrical energy.
All this energy comes from chemical reactions.
And all of it comes from the food you eat

To understand how this energy is released, think of muscle cells. Their energy is usually provided from the glucose present in the cells. If, however, the cells run out of glucose they will call on their immediate reserve - a substance called glycogen. This is broken down to glucose again for more energy.

If they run out of this immediate store, they have to make an emergency call via the brain to your fat deposits.

The brain signals the release of hormones into your bloodstream. They trigger off chemical reactions inside the fat cells, which cause the stored fat to be broken down into a smaller form, in which they can travel in the bloodstream to the muscles. The fats are then burnt in the muscle cells to give the necessary chemical energy.

Metabolism
This is how weight is controlled in principle. But in practice, of course, many people have thin friends who can eat and eat without getting fat.

My husband devours everything in sight including sweets and chocolate *ad lib* and is decidedly slim. My daughter lives on fresh air but is like me in build and has inherited my problems.

Some slimmers are convinced that there must be a reason for this.

Why do people leading comparable lives remain thin and others put on weight at an alarming rate?

The answer is probably in the working of the body's metabolism. This word covers all the chemical changes which take place in all the cells of your body. Metabolism is the growth of new tissues, the breakdown of old tissues and the production of energy.

Among medical experts there are two schools of thought about whether metabolism has a role in creating a tendency towards fatness.

Everyone is agreed that you will get fat if the amount of energy you take in as food and drink is greater than the amount of energy you use up. So fat people have, at some time or another, eaten too much for their own requirements.

Some experts think that that's all there is to it. On the other hand, there are those that believe that there are some people who have never eaten an abnormally large amount but have, for some reason, become fat.

Every function of the body needs energy.
Your muscles contract to provide mechanical energy.
Your nerves use electrical energy.
All this energy comes from chemical reactions.
And all of it comes from the food you eat.

To understand how this energy is released, think of muscle cells. Their energy is usually provided from the glucose present in the cells. If, however, the cells run out of glucose they will call on their immediate reserve - a substance called glycogen. This is broken down to glucose again for more energy.

If they run out of this immediate store, they have to make an emergency call via the brain to your fat deposits.

The brain signals the release of hormones into your bloodstream. They trigger off chemical reactions inside the fat cells, which cause the stored fat to be broken down into a smaller form, in which they can travel in the bloodstream to the muscles. The fats are then burnt in the muscle cells to give the necessary chemical energy.

Metabolism
This is how weight is controlled in principle. But in practice, of course, many people have thin friends who can eat and eat without getting fat.

My husband devours everything in sight including sweets and chocolate *ad lib* and is decidedly slim. My daughter lives on fresh air but is like me in build and has inherited my problems.

Some slimmers are convinced that there must be a reason for this.

Why do people leading comparable lives remain thin and others put on weight at an alarming rate.

The answer is probably in the working of the body's metabolism. This word covers all the chemical changes which take place in all the cells of your body. Metabolism is the growth of new tissues, the breakdown of old tissues and the production of energy.

Among medical experts there are two schools of thought about whether metabolism has a role in creating a tendency towards fatness.

Everyone is agreed that you will get fat if the amount of energy you take in as food and drink is greater than the amount of energy you use up. So fat people have, at some time or another, eaten too much for their own requirements.

Some experts think that that's all there is to it. On the other hand, there are those that believe that there are some people who have never eaten an abnormally large amount but have, for some reason, become fat.

Different degrees of emphasis for the same piece of copy

Italic has too little contrast with the surrounding text to give much emphasis. This is not helped by the lack of extra space.

Text-size bold (below) is much clearer, particularly when the paragraphs are pulled out and given their own space.

The same weight but a larger size also works quite well.

EVERY FUNCTION OF THE BODY NEEDS ENERGY

Your muscles contract to provide mechanical energy. Your nerves use electrical energy. All this energy comes from chemical reactions.

AND ALL OF IT COMES FROM THE FOOD YOU EAT

To understand how this energy is released, think of muscle cells. Their energy is usually provided from the glucose present in the cells. If, however, the cells run out of glucose they will call on their immediate reserve - a substance called glycogen. This is broken down to glucose again for more energy. *If they run out of this immediate store, they have to make an emergency call via the brain to your fat deposits.* The brain signals the release of hormones into your bloodstream. They trigger off chemical reactions inside the fat cells, which cause the stored fat to be broken down into a smaller form, in which they can travel in the bloodstream to the muscles. *The fats are then burnt in the muscle cells to give the necessary chemical energy.*

Metabolism
This is how weight is controlled in principle. But in practice, of course, many people have thin friends who can eat and eat without getting fat.

'My husband devours everything in sight including sweets and chocolate ad lib and is decidedly slim. My daughter lives on fresh air but is like me in build and has inherited my problems.'

Some slimmers are convinced that there must be a reason for this.

Why do people leading comparable lives remain thin and others put on weight at an alarming rate?

The answer is probably in the working of the body's metabolism. This word covers all the chemical changes which take place in all the cells of your body. Metabolism is the growth of new tissues, the breakdown of old tissues and the production of energy.

Among medical experts there are two schools of thought about whether metabolism has a role in creating a tendency towards fatness. Everyone is agreed that you will get fat if the amount of energy you take in as food and drink is greater than the amount of energy you use up. *So fat people have, at some time or another, eaten too much for their own requirements.*

Some experts think that that's all there is to it. On the other hand, there are those that believe that there are some people who have never eaten an abnormally large amount but have, for some reason, become fat.

Every function of the body needs energy. Your muscles contract to provide mechanical energy. Your nerves use electrical energy. All this energy comes from chemical reactions.
And all of it comes from the food you eat

To understand how this energy is released, think of muscle cells. Their energy is usually provided from the glucose present in the cells. If, however, the cells run out of glucose they will call on their immediate reserve - a substance called glycogen. This is broken down to glucose again for more energy.

If they run out of this immediate store, they have to make an emergency call via the brain to your fat deposits.

The brain signals the release of hormones into your bloodstream. They trigger off chemical reactions inside the fat cells, which cause the stored fat to be broken down into a smaller form, in which they can travel in the bloodstream to the muscles. The fats are then burnt in the muscle cells to give the necessary chemical energy.

Metabolism
This is how weight is controlled in principle. But in practice, of course, many people have thin friends who can eat and eat without getting fat.

'My husband devours everything in sight including sweets and chocolate *ad lib* and is decidedly slim. My daughter lives on fresh air but is like me in build and has inherited my problems.'

Some slimmers are convinced that there must be a reason for this.

Why do people leading comparable lives remain thin and others put on weight at an alarming rate?

The answer is probably in the working of the body's metabolism. This word covers all the chemical changes which take place in all the cells of your body. Metabolism is the growth of new tissues, the breakdown of old tissues and the production of energy.

Among medical experts there are two schools of thought about whether metabolism has a role in creating a tendency towards fatness.

Everyone is agreed that you will get fat if the amount of energy you take in as food and drink is greater than the amount of energy you use up. So fat people have, at some time or another, eaten too much for their own requirements.

Some experts think that that's all there is to it. On the other hand, there are those that believe that there are some people who have never eaten an abnormally large amount but have, for some reason, become fat.

Every function of the body needs energy.
Your muscles contract to provide mechanical energy.
Your nerves use electrical energy.
All this energy comes from chemical reactions.
And all of it comes from the food you eat.

To understand how this energy is released, think of muscle cells. Their energy is usually provided from the glucose present in the cells. If, however, the cells run out of glucose they will call on their immediate reserve - a substance called glycogen. This is broken down to glucose again for more energy. If they run out of this immediate store, they have to make an emergency call via the brain to your fat deposits. The brain signals the release of hormones into your bloodstream. They trigger off chemical reactions inside the fat cells, which cause the stored fat to be broken down into a smaller form, in which they can travel in the bloodstream to the muscles. The fats are then burnt in the muscle cells to give the necessary chemical energy.

Metabolism
This is how weight is controlled in principle. But in practice, of course, many people have thin friends who can eat and eat without getting fat.

'My husband devours everything in sight including sweets and chocolate *ad lib* and is decidedly slim. My daughter lives on fresh air but is like me in build and has inherited my problems.'

Some slimmers are convinced that there must be a reason for this.

Why do people leading comparable lives remain thin and others put on weight at an alarming rate?

The answer is probably in the working of the body's metabolism. This word covers all the chemical changes which take place in all the cells of your body. Metabolism is the growth of new tissues, the breakdown of old tissues and the production of energy.

Among medical experts there are two schools of thought about whether metabolism has a role in creating a tendency towards fatness.

Everyone is agreed that you will get fat if the amount of energy you take in as food and drink is greater than the amount of energy you use up. So fat people have, at some time or another, eaten too much for their own requirements.

Some experts think that that's all there is to it. On the other hand, there are those that believe that there are some people who have never eaten an abnormally large amount but have, for some reason, become fat.

Indenting

Indenting lines, that is preceding them with a space, can be a useful device for giving emphasis or indicating that a particular piece of information is separate from another.

Paragraph indents

Opening a paragraph with a space at the beginning of the first line is a well established convention which most people will understand. However such conventions are not sacrosanct and it is possible to achieve the same end in other ways.

Methods of indenting should take into account the typographic style of the rest of the document.

For example, if the text is ranged left. as this is, giving a ragged right-hand edge, then paragraphs indented on the left give a ragged effect on both sides. It is better, if you have the room, to put a line space between the paragraphs and set them all to the left. If, on the other hand, the text is set justified so that all the lines are the same length, then paragraph indenting is essential.

A double space indent is normally enough. Sometimes a very exaggerated indent is used, as much as halfway along the line. This is something of an affectation which can be irritating. In any case it should be reserved for text with very long paragraphs or for section headings only.

There should be no indent after a subheading.

Conventional paragraph indent works well for justified text.

Generally speaking one can say that internal information is primarily produced 'in house', whereas external information is sent to 'specialists' for production.

Information produced 'in house' for internal use is usually typographically inferior to externally produced information. This is due to less sophisticated production tools.

The introduction of the 'personal computer' into organisations for the purpose of text production, both internal and external, is the first manifestation of the new technology with which we are concerned.

Very exaggerated indents are suited only to copy with very long paragraphs - not recommended.

Generally speaking one can say that internal information is primarily produced 'in house', whereas external information is sent to 'specialists' for production.

Information produced 'in house' for internal use is usually typographically inferior to externally produced information. This is due to less sophisticated production tools.

The introduction of the 'personal computer' into organisations for the purpose of text production, both internal and external, is the first manifestation of the new technology with which we are concerned.

Paragraph indents with ranged left setting give a very ragged column...

Generally speaking one can say that internal information is primarily produced 'in house', whereas external information is sent to 'specialists' for production.

Information produced 'in house' for internal use is usually typographically inferior to externally produced information. This is due to less sophisticated production tools.

The introduction of the 'personal computer' into organisations for the purpose of text production, both internal and external, is the first manifestation of the new technology with which we are concerned.

...full out to the left with a line space between paragraphs looks better.

Generally speaking one can say that internal information is primarily produced 'in house', whereas external information is sent to 'specialists' for production.

Information produced 'in house' for internal use is usually typographically inferior to externally produced information. This is due to less sophisticated production tools.

The introduction of the 'personal computer' into organisations for the purpose of text production, both internal and external, is the first manifestation of the new technology with which we are concerned.

Indenting text

Text can be indented to show that it is in some way different from the main copy (see *Quoted Passages*) but avoid using indents to indicate sub and sub-sub paragraphs. This is a bureaucratic convention that can be very confusing to the reader. There may be times when these conventions are very well established as in some scientific works but they are not suitable for general publications.

Individual paragraphs can be picked out by using a marker such as a number or a blob and indenting all the rest of the paragraph. This is called a 'hanging indent'.

Using a dash (-) as a marker always seems a rather feeble hangover from the typewriter. If you really want to emphasise a paragraph then a blob ( ) will be more effective.

Numbering a series of paragraphs is only necessary if they are either referred to elsewhere in the text, or a specific number of points has been indicated: 'There are three reasons why ...' followed by three numbered paragraphs. Cross-reference is better done by paragraph numbering throughout.

If numbers are used keep them as simple as possible. Arabic numerals with the minimum of brackets and other punctuation. This is particularly important when the numbers run to more than five.
(7 is a lot clearer than vii).

Keep the tens and units under one another and follow the number with a clear space. I like to leave out all unnecessary punctuation but some editors insist on a stop after paragraph numbers. I usually agree because there will be more important things to fight over .

Indents in Wonderland

The complicated system of indents and sub-paragraphs in a Government paper have great significance for the initiated but are confusing to the average reader.

Clements Lane
between a point 18.29 metres north-east of the north-eastern kerb-line of Ilford Lane and the south-western kerb-line of Clements Road.

Clements Road
(1) between the south-eastern kerb-line of High Road, Ilford at its south-westernmost junction with Clements Road and a point 21.34 metres south-east of that kerb-line;
(2) the north-eastern arm, between a point 18.29 metres south-east of the south-eastern kerb-line of High Road, Ilford and its junction with the south-eastern arm of Clements Road;
(3) the south-eastern arm,
(*a*) the north-west side,
(i) between its junction with the south-western arm of Clements Road and the south-western kerb-line of Chadwick Road;
(ii) between the north-eastern kerb-line of Oakfield Road and its junction with the north-eastern arm of Clements Road;
(*b*) the south-east side,
(i) between its junction with the south-western arm of Clements Road and the south-western kerb-line of Handforth Road;
(ii) between a point 14.00 metres south-west of a point opposite the south-western kerb-line of Oakfield Road and its junction with the north-eastern arm of Clements Road.

High Road, Ilford
between its junctions with Ilford Lane and Cranbrook Road and a point 18.29 metres south-west of the south-western kerb-line of Clements Road at is north-easternmost junction

Hanging indent with a bold subhead.

If you have health, a great craving for adventure, at least a moderate fortune and can set your heart on a definite object, which old travellers do not think impracticable, then - travel by all means.

Reputed dangers of travel. A young man of good constitution who is bound on an enterprise sanctioned by experienced travellers, does not run very great risks. Let those who doubt refer to the various expeditions encouraged by the Royal Geographical Society and they will see how few deaths have occurred; and of those deaths how small a proportion among young travellers.

Advantages of travel. It is no slight advantage to a young man to have the opportunity for distinction which travel affords. If he plans his journey among scenes and places likely to interest the stay-at-home public, he will probably achieve a reputation that might well be envied by wiser men who have not had his opportunities.

The scientific advantages of travel are enormous to a man prepared to profit by them. He sees Nature working by herself, without the interference of human intelligence; and he sees her from new points of view; he also has

Hanging indent with blobs

If you have health, a great craving for adventure, at least a moderate fortune and can set your heart on a definite object, which old travellers do not think impracticable, then - travel by all means.

Reputed dangers of travel. A young man of good constitution who is bound on an enterprise sanctioned by experienced travellers, does not run very great risks. Let those who doubt refer to the expeditions encouraged by the Royal Geographical Society and they will see how few deaths have occurred; and of those deaths how small a proportion among young travellers.

Advantages of travel. It is no slight advantage to a young man to have the opportunity for distinction which travel affords. If he plans his journey among scenes and places likely to interest the stay-at-home public, he will probably achieve a reputation that might well be envied by wiser men who have not had his opportunities.

The scientific advantages of travel are enormous to a man prepared to profit

Rules, boxes and other devices

Most of these devices serve to separate text. Whether or not they give emphasis or merely divide one piece of copy from another depends on how you use them.

An exaggerated example

The horizontal rules in column 1 emphasise to the reader the three main subjects to be dealt with on the following pages.

Rules

In headings rules can be used to give drama and vigour. They can also be useful in containing very long, wordy chapter headings, particularly if they run over more than one column of say a three-column layout.

Heading rules can be heavier than rules used within the text but they should not dominate the typeface.

In the text rules make a barrier. This can be used effectively but there must be a good reason why the reader should be stopped in his tracks.

Rules used within a column will tend to divide and separate whereas used across two columns they will divide from the text above but link the columns below.

Rules can be used to emphasise longer passages; the degree of emphasis can be increased by using bold text.

As with other devices of this kind, they will be more effective if they are used sparingly. Use the same weight of rule throughout. Degrees of importance indicated by weight of rule will be lost on most readers. If you do need to use various weights of rule make them clearly different, otherwise it will look like a mistake.

Ruled-off text must be positioned with care. If it is not part of the surrounding copy then find a 'natural break' to drop it into. If it is continuous with the text then make sure it falls within a column - don't break it from one column to the next.

State retirement pensions

Even if your retirement seems a long way off, what you do now could affect your pension in the future.

Planning for retirement ought to start as early as leaving school. At that age it may seem absurd to worry about what will happen to you at the end of your working life - and many people don't give the matter enough thought until they are well into middle age.

How much State pension you will get will depend on your paying National Insurance contributions over many years.

There are three main retirement pensions from the state:

1 **Basic** (flat rate) pension

2 **Additional** (earnings related)

3 **Graduated** pension

The basic pension is paid to everyone - including married women - with enough contributions. The standard pension rate is laid down each year by the Government. If you have too few contributions to qualify for the full amount, you might still be able to get a proportion of it.
You can qualify for an additional pension only for periods spent working for an employer. But if you are a member of a 'contracted out' pension scheme see box. You cannot contribute to the additional pension scheme while you are self-employed or not working. The amount you get depends on your earnings and how many years you have contributed.

Graduated pensions are a relic of the state scheme which existed from 1961 to 1975. They were a simpler version of today's additional pension scheme but the amounts paid out are fairly small.

Contracting out

A pension scheme you belong to through your job may be 'contracted out' of the state additional pension scheme. For the period you belong to a contracted out scheme your employer takes over the job of paying you a pension on retirement, broadly equivalent to the additional pension you would have otherwise got from the state. This part of your pension - called the guaranteed minimum pension (GMP) - is increased in line with earnings in the economy as a whole, up until your retirement.

The boxes are positioned so that the reader is in no doubt that the main text continues from the middle of column 2 to the top of column 4.

The 'example' needs to be separated from the text but does not warrant a box - horizontal rules work better.

The earnings rule

As long as you count as officially retired you can earn more than £65 a week and still receive the state pension. But you may lose some or all of your basic pension under the earnings rule.

- For weekly earnings over £65 and up to £69 you lose 5p of pension for each additional 10p earned.
- For earnings over £69 you lose 5p of pension for each additional 5p earned.

The reduction applies to the whole of your basic pension but does not affect the additional or graduated pension.

State pensions may not seem very large, compared with your earnings, but they are a valuable source of retirement income because they are 'inflation proofed'. They are increased each November by the change in the Retail Price Index over the 12 months to the preceding May. There are also non-contributory pensions available to retired people mainly on low incomes.

When you can get state pension

You can get state retirement pension only if you have reached the official pensionable age of 65 for men, or 60 for women. If you retire from work before this age you will still have to wait until 65 or 60 to get any state pension.

Once you reach the age of 70 (men) or 65 (women) you get your pension regardless of any work

Example

If you qualify for a full basic pension of £34.05 a week, but you earn £101.05 a week, you get no basic pension at all.

Similarly extra pension you get for your wife will be reduced by 5p for every 10p she earns over £45 a week, up to £49, and by 5p for every 5p she earns over £49 - this on top of any reduction due to your earnings.

If a pension based on your contribution is paid to your wife, it will not be affected by your earnings but it will be affected if her own earnings exceed £65 a week.

If you are a widow between the ages of 60 and 65 doing paid work, you might do better to carry on getting widow's pension, which is not affected by earnings, rather than a retirement pension.

Investment income does not affect the amount of basic pension you get.

Boxes

Boxed copy is material which is usually relevant to the contents of the rest of the page but can be read separately and in isolation from it. For this reason each box should be given a heading or subtitle of its own. If this doesn't seem appropriate then check whether you really want a box or whether horizontal rules would do the job better.

Boxes can greatly affect the pace and 'colour' of a page and they should be positioned carefully. They do not have to be adjacent to relevant copy within the main text but they should at least appear on the same spread. Treat them as you would illustrations. As with ruled-off copy, boxes can break the flow of text if they are not skillfully placed. If they come in the middle of a column the reader may not be sure where the main text continues.

There is no limit to the length of copy contained in a box but if it does occupy a whole column or half a page, a single rule in the gutter (the space between columns) or across the page can work just as well.

A box should be the same width as the column or pair of columns it sits in. So the text will have to be set to a narrower width to allow for the thickness of the rule and the space between the box and the text. Always allow a comfortable space round the text - at least the equivalent of a double indent - otherwise it will look pinched and uncomfortable.

Although it can look decorative it is not often a good idea to box whole pages. The visual effect is to constrict the page and lose the benefit of the surrounding white space. There is also the very real risk that if the pages are trimmed very slightly off-square, the straight line of the box, coming near the edge of the page, will make the error more obvious.

Tint panels

Tint panels are another way of separating copy. Because they are clearly different from boxes they can be used to separate different sorts of text or to give emphasis in a different way.

Not all word processors may be able to produce tints. They can be added by hand later to hard copy providing you allow for them during keyboarding by setting to a narrower measure.

Placing tint panels on the page is similar to positioning boxes and the same advice on not over-using them applies.

A grey tint panel behind black type will weaken the text. So make sure the type is strong enough to take it. A dot tint for example will break down the definition of fine serifs and a very dark tint may obliterate the type altogether. If the print is going to be all black, use a fine dot giving a light tint. If, on the other hand, you are going to print the tint as a second colour then the tint will need to be heavier to hold the colour.

Dot tints can give an unsightly ragged edge to the panel. This can be avoided by putting a fine box round it. A heavier line will give more power to the whole panel but it can make it look funereal. In any case having decided on the weight of rule use the same one throughout.

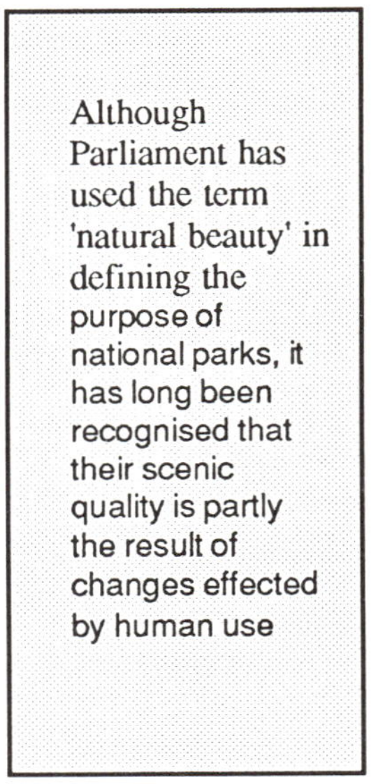

Type stands up quite well on a light tint but a sanserif fares better than a serifed face.

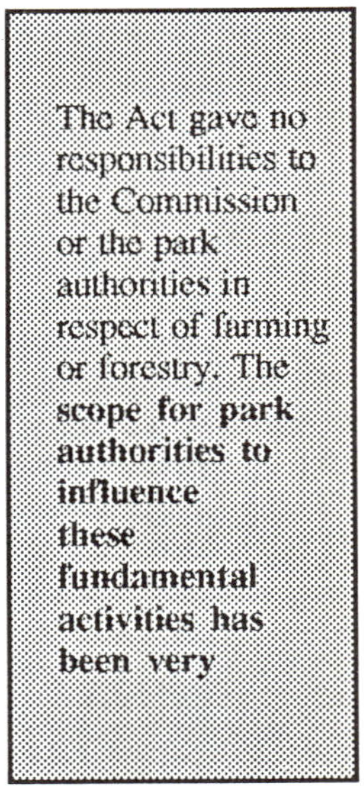

Too dark a tint kills the lettering although bold helps.

Colour allows the use of a darker tint.

Enlargement shows how much the form of the letter is broken up by the tint.

Tint panels without borders look less overpowering, but tints with round corners can have a ragged edge.

Blobs and arrows

Sometimes ordinary subheadings don't seem to be enough and more graphic signposts are called for in the text. Their size and vigour will depend on their context but remember that if they are well used the reader will rely on them as a guide so it is important to use them consistently and logically.

Blobs or cannon balls are a fairly familiar device used mostly to emphasise particular paragraphs.

● They can be set into the text like a run-on heading so that they act as a pointer without giving too much emphasis.

- Or they can be treated as a hanging indent, which means that they stick out clearly into the margin and draw more attention.

- Blobs can be very powerful against the adjacent text so they should be smaller than the capitals.

- Always use the same size of blob throughout one document and use it for the same degree of emphasis. Differences between one size of blob and another will be hard for the reader to recognise and may be confusing.

Arrows are a much more powerful image and should be used more discriminately.

Arrows can be used either to draw very insistent attention to a particular piece of text or to link one piece of text with another.

If arrows are used too freely they will lose their impact. If there are a lot of points to emphasise it is better to use something less powerful like a blob and reserve the arrow for an occasional important highlight.

Initial letters

Big capital letters are sometimes used at the beginning of a paragraph. Their purpose is both to draw the reader's eye to the point where the text begins and to be decorative.

As there is often only one place on the page to begin reading, their use is mostly decorative.

Like all primarily decorative elements they should be used with care and sparingly; preferably at the beginning of a chapter only.

There are several ways of treating them, all of which take time and care. A badly placed initial is very unsightly and can make it quite difficult to decipher the first word.

Raised initials in which the letter sits proud above the first line of text. This may appear to be a fairly simple way of doing it but it requires more than a simple keyboard operation.

Dropped initials which occupy the first few lines of text. These again have to be handled with some skill particularly when using letters with an irregular outline like 'T' and 'L'.

In bookwork and in other suitable documents it sometimes helps to put the first line into capitals of the same size as the text.

Other variations include fitting the letter onto a rectangular tint or reversing out of a solid. This avoids the problem of irregular shaped letters, but it can divorce the initial from the rest of the word - see example.

Raised letters in which the letter sits proud above the first line of text. This may appear to be a fairly simple way of doing it but it requires more than a simple keyboard operation.

Dropped initials which occupy the first few lines of text. These again have to be handled with some skill particularly when using letters which have an irregular outline such as T and L.

IN BOOKS AND SOME other documents it sometimes helps to put the first line in capitals of the same size as the text

Your arrangement of the layout is crucial to the understanding of the text. Initial letters contained in a rectangle avoid the problem of irregular shaped letters but divorce the initial from the rest of the word.

Quoted passages

How lengthy quotations within the text are dealt with will depend on their purpose in the document and the way in which you want the reader to perceive them.

If the quotation is included to illustrate a point or support an argument in a prose text, then it is probably best to use one of the conventions established for bookwork. If the quotations are a main feature and need emphasising to the casual reader then a more displayed arrangement may be necessary.

Quotes of a few words from other documents, that appear within the text are best identified by using 'single quotes' reserving "double quotes" for quotations within a quoted passage.

Longer quotations need to be separated from the body of the text to make it clear that they are not the author's own words. Some of the ways of doing this are illustrated on the right.

It is important to use the same method throughout the document. Having settled on a technique for handling quotes within the text, it is a good idea to establish a standard that is used by everyone in the same organisation.

Displayed quotes
There are any number of ways in which to display passages of direct speech in a text. The method used will depend on their frequency and importance.

If the number on the page is few but significant, then you can afford to use a fairly powerful displayed quote. Such features can be decorative but also overpowering. Too many on one spread will dominate the layout and readers may find it difficult to see what is going on.

Quote in the same size as the main text, indented with quote marks.
No extra space between the text and the quotation.

Boswell records that on 29 September he ran off from Margaret in a bad humour, on 3 October she was displeased to read in his journal about the chamber maids, on 7 October he was quite well, and on 10 October he got drunk and was horrible to her, being very ill the next day. The entry of 13 October brings him to the low point of this particular period:
'Exceedingly ill; as dreary and horrible as ever. Called [on] Grange; groaned and could hardly speak. Wretched, wretched ... quite sunk. Bad cold appeared.'
A few days later he set off on a duty visit to Auchinleck, which did not improve his mood.

Space inserted above and below the quote, full out to the left, no quote marks.

Boswell records that on 29 September he ran off from Margaret in a bad humour, on 3 October she was displeased to read in his journal about the chamber maids, on 7 October he was quite well, and on 10 October he got drunk and was horrible to her, being very ill the next day. The entry of 13 October brings him to the low point of this particular period:

Exceedingly ill; as dreary and horrible as ever. Called [on] Grange; groaned and could hardly speak. Wretched, wretched ... quite sunk. Bad cold appeared.

A few days later he set off on a duty visit to Auchinleck, which did not improve his mood.

The same as above but with the quotation set a size smaller.
My own preference.

Boswell records that on 29 September he ran off from Margaret in a bad humour, on 3 October she was displeased to read in his journal about the chamber maids, on 7 October he was quite well, and on 10 October he got drunk and was horrible to her, being very ill the next day. The entry of 13 October brings him to the low point of this particular period:

Exceedingly ill; as dreary and horrible as ever. Called [on] Grange; groaned and could hardly speak. Wretched, wretched ... quite sunk. Bad cold appeared.

A few days later he set off on a duty visit to Auchinleck, which did not improve his mood.

The careful use of space and type size can do the job just as well and not leave the reader with the feeling that he is being shouted at from all over the page.

The method of display should be the same on a single spread or through the same article, but it is quite legitimate to use different techniques in the same publication.

However, making such displays takes quite a long time on a PC so you might want to store a small repertoire of quotation frames to call up when they are needed.

Because of the job situation where I live, I've been offered early retirement. If I take it will I get a state pension?

Because of the job situation where I live, I've been offered early retirement. If I take it will I get a state pension?

Because of the job situation where I live, I've been offered early retirement. If I take it will I get a state pension ?

Because of the job situation where I live, I've been offered early retirement. If I take it will I get a state pension?

Mrs Cakebread lives in Ipswich, and though she has several supermarkets within a mile or so of her home, she prefers to drive the ten miles into Woodbridge to shop at Smallbones. Why the additional journey?

"I've been going there for years and in the big supermarkets I can't find anything. They seem to move things around ."

Mrs C. shops fortnightly and buys for a family of three. She also has a full-time job.

"Other places might be cheaper but I don't have time to shop around."

Another thing that Mrs Cakebread likes about the small shop is that she can buy the other things she needs.

"The supermarkets don't stock paraffin and the bread tastes nicer."

If Mrs Cakebread found time to shop around she might save £6 on every £40 shopping bill but, like many other people, she says:

"Shopping isn't just a matter of money. Convenience and less obvious things like just feeling comfortable in the shop... they're part of it too."

Preliminary pages

This is the name - usually shortened to 'prelims' - given to the opening pages of any book or other document before the text proper starts.

Prelims usually include:
half-title
title
imprint or bibliographical details
contents
list of illustrations
introduction

These, together with a few others such as 'dedication', have a traditional order in bookwork but the designer of more ephemeral documents should not be inhibited by that. Prelim pages are one part of a document that can be expanded or contracted with the least damage to the sense of the text.

The opening pages of a document are often vital in getting readers to turn over and read on. So the contents may well be part of the title page or even the cover, and the bibliographical details - date and place of publication - although necessary, might be relegated to the back page.

Half-title This is normally the first page of the first section of a book and so is the one that gets glued onto the endpaper which attaches it to the binding. This opening half-title serves no real purpose outside bookwork. (For half titles separating sections within a document see *Section dividers* below.)

Title page This is usually the first page of a document after the cover. It will invariably carry the title and usually the names of the author(s), illustrator and publisher. But other information, such as the contents, can be included. It is usually a compromise between available space and fitness for purpose. If there are a lot of spare pages to be used up the

Below
half-title and
imprint page.

Title and
contents page.

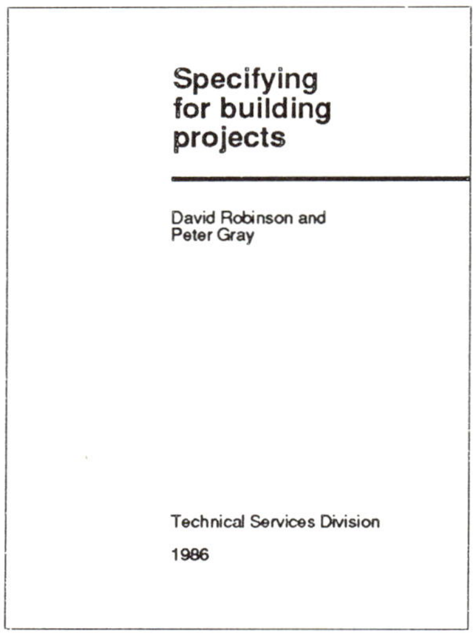

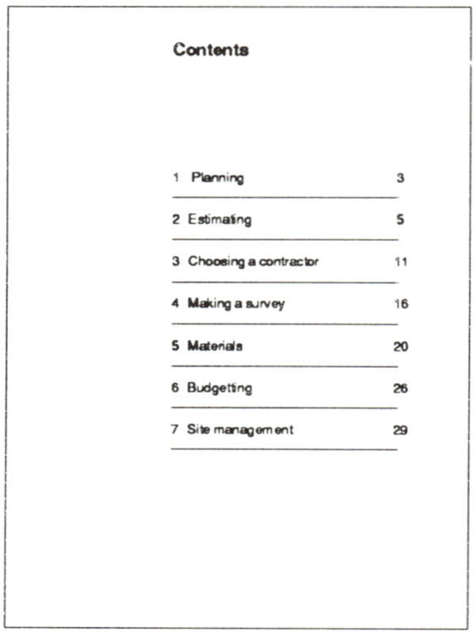

Title page copy can include more than just the title of the publication.

The layout of the title page should be in the same style and on the same grid as the rest of the document.

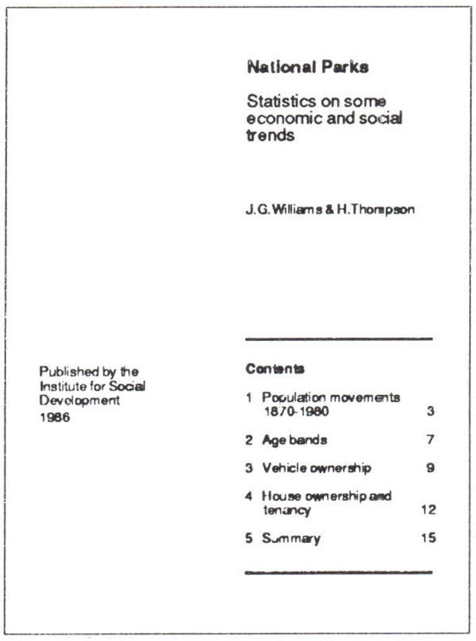

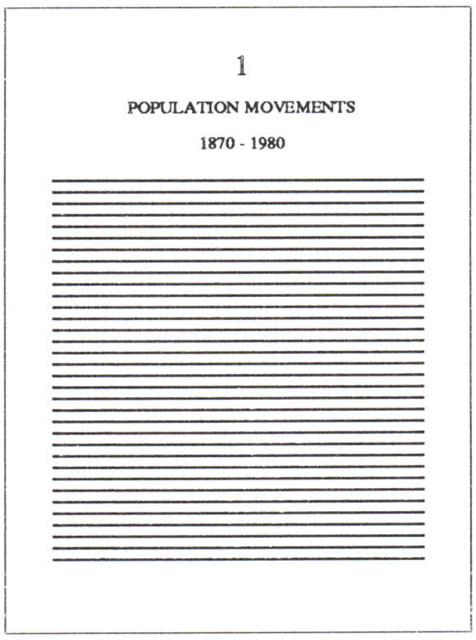

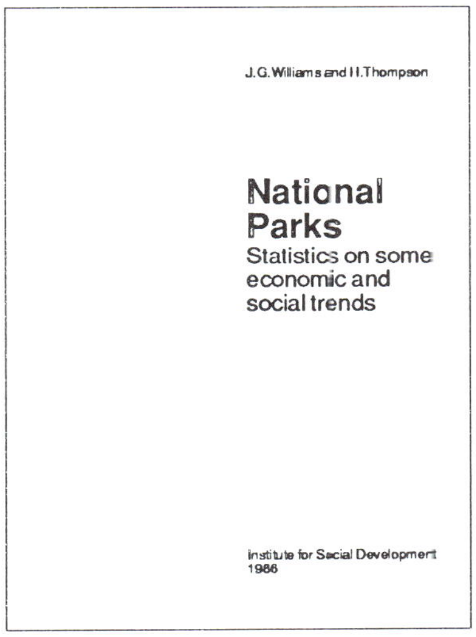

contents will probably have a right-hand page to itself but if space is very short then the title page and contents may both be used to make the cover itself.

The layout of the title page should be in keeping with that of the rest of the document. So if the text layout is asymmetric the title page should be too. If the chapters all start at a constant level on the page then it may be convenient to have the title of the publication in the same position on the page. It always helps the continuity of the document if the title page grid is the same as for the rest of the pages.

There is no fixed order for the information that goes on the title page. Remember that the reader's eye will not necessarily go straight to the top of the page but is more likely to start about a quarter of the way down.

When arranging a title page avoid getting the longest line at the top of the page or below the visual centre. This applies to both centred and asymmetric layouts, or any displayed text.

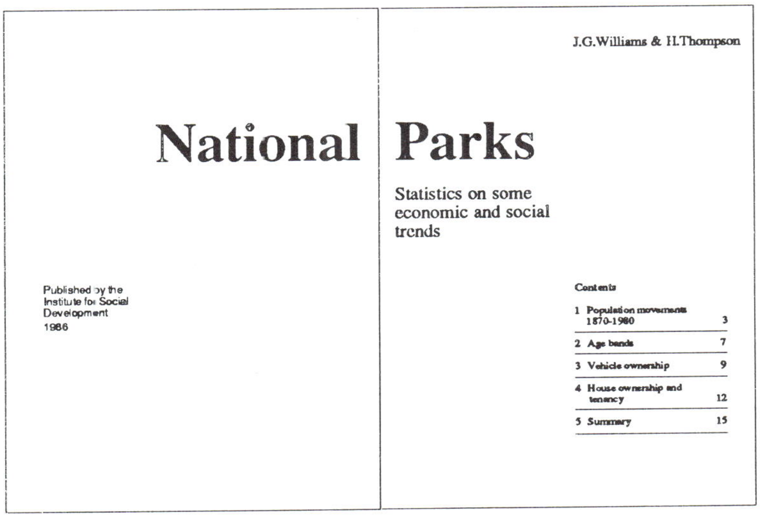

Title pages do not have to be confined to a single, right-hand page. They can occupy a whole spread if the binding is suitable.

Bibliographical details or imprint These are essential in any document. It is important for readers to know when it was published and in which edition and who holds the copyright, but this information does not have to be displayed prominently. In books the normal position is on the back of the title page but it can go into any convenient space in the prelims or at the end of the document.

Contents These may vary from a simple list of chapters to an elaborate, annotated list with subheadings. A lot will depend on how you expect the reader to use it.

A very simple text may need only a very basic contents list or even none at all but in many documents the contents can be used as a guide to the reader. If the contents has more of a selling job to do then it may be necessary to display it prominently with a brief summary of the contents of each chapter.

The contents list does not have to be set to the full page width. The page number should not be so far away from the chapter title that the eye has difficulty in linking the two. Use the vertical grid as a guide to a suitable width. For instance if the pages are set in double column then the contents might be the width of one column only.

If there are section as well as chapter divisions they can be emphasised or set as side headings.

It sometimes helps to set rules across the page to help to carry the eye along. Leader lines - rows of dots - are rather fussy and look a bit archaic.

If the contents page is very complicated particular attention will have to be paid to articulating space and the use of different weights of type.

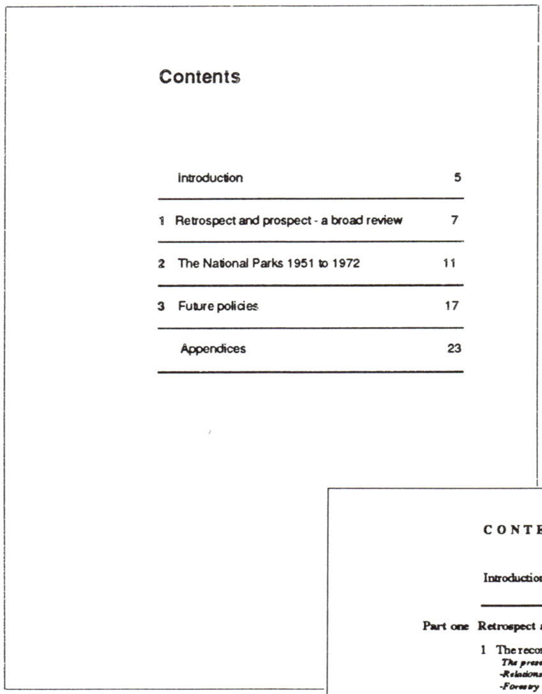
Contents

Introduction 5
1 Retrospect and prospect - a broad review 7
2 The National Parks 1951 to 1972 11
3 Future policies 17
Appendices 23

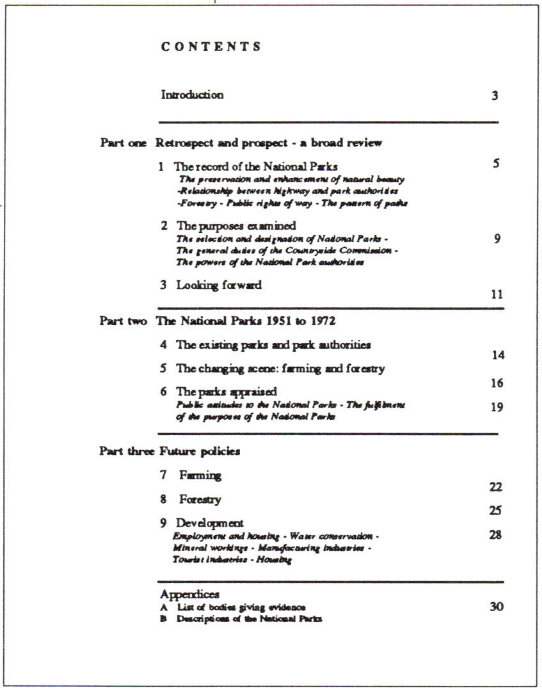
CONTENTS

Introduction 3

Part one Retrospect and prospect - a broad review
1 The record of the National Parks 5
The preservation and enhancement of natural beauty -Relationship between highway and park authorities -Forestry - Public rights of way - The pattern of paths
2 The purposes examined 9
The selection and designation of National Parks - The general duties of the Countryside Commission - The powers of the National Park authorities
3 Looking forward 11

Part two The National Parks 1951 to 1972
4 The existing parks and park authorities 14
5 The changing scene: farming and forestry 16
6 The parks appraised 19
Public attitudes to the National Parks - The fulfilment of the purposes of the National Parks

Part three Future policies
7 Farming 22
8 Forestry 25
9 Development 28
Employment and housing - Water conservation - Mineral workings - Manufacturing industries - Tourist industries - Housing

Appendices 30
A List of bodies giving evidence
B Descriptions of the National Parks

The contents list can be very simple, very detailed or displayed, depending on how the publication is to be used and the reader it is aimed at.

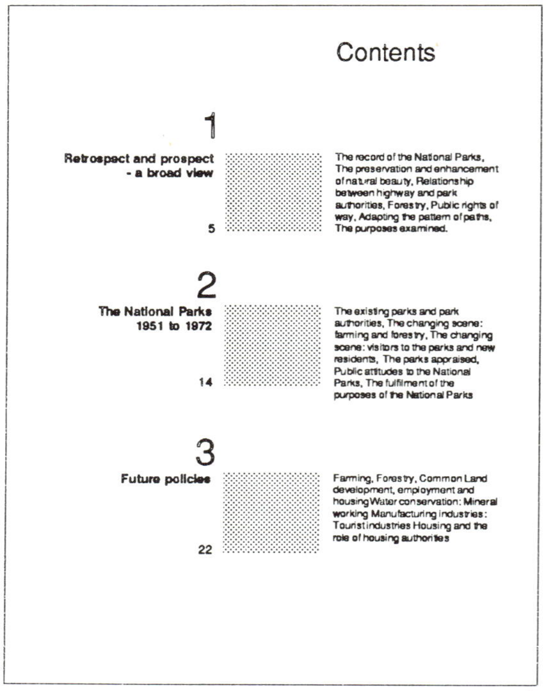
Contents

1
Retrospect and prospect - a broad view
5
The record of the National Parks, The preservation and enhancement of natural beauty, Relationship between highway and park authorities, Forestry, Public rights of way, Adapting the pattern of paths, The purposes examined.

2
The National Parks 1951 to 1972
14
The existing parks and park authorities, The changing scene: farming and forestry, The changing scene: visitors to the parks and new residents, The parks appraised, Public attitudes to the National Parks, The fulfilment of the purposes of the National Parks

3
Future policies
22
Farming, Forestry, Common Land development, employment and housing Water conservation: Mineral working Manufacturing industries: Tourist industries Housing and the role of housing authorities

List of illustrations If this is needed treat it simply. As with the contents don't feel obliged to use the full width of the page unless the captions are very long.

Introduction Be sure that an Introduction or Foreword/ Preface is really needed. Many readers skip it as a matter of course. It sometimes helps to give it a different pace from the rest of the text by setting it in a larger size or to a different measure, but let the measure follow the logic of the grid.

Section dividers If a document is divided into sections it may be convenient to separate them with half-title pages. To be effective these must each appear on a right-hand page preferably followed by a blank verso page.

Section dividers can simply carry the number and title of the ensuing section but they can also carry a contents list for that section.

If the publication is to be saddle-stitched (see *Binding*) or if there is to be a very large edition, then the divider pages will almost certainly have to be printed at the same time and on the same material as the rest of the book. If the binding is to be some form of single sheet or loose leaf method then it may be possible to use heavier paper or thin card for the dividers. If the way in which the document is to be used calls for a very marked division between sections then different colours can be introduced.

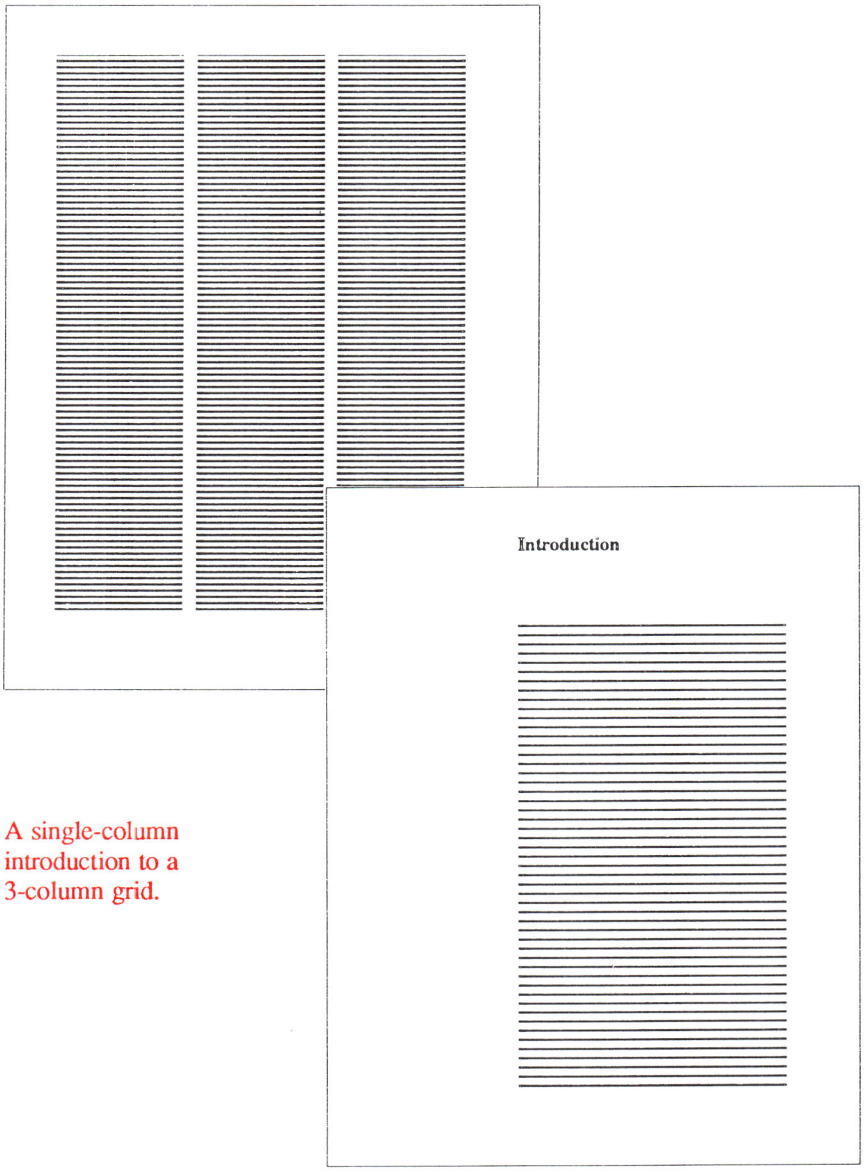

A single-column introduction to a 3-column grid.

If the information on a section divider is placed to the right, readers will find it more easily as they thumb through.

Tabular setting

Before you begin setting up a table look at the material and decide what information the table has to convey and how the reader is going to use it.

All tables work on two axes - vertical and horizontal - but they don't all present information in the same way. In a statistical table for instance, the reader may want to compare one figure against another whereas in a timetable the need is to identify a particular time or destination. It is these considerations which dictate the direction in which a table is read.

Most tables have a primary reading direction, either vertical or horizontal. That is, you either read across the table first and then up and down or you start by running your finger up the table and then read across.

Exceptions are tables such as those which give distances between towns. The answer lies at the point where the two axes meet and one direction is no more important than the other. But most tables have a fairly clear bias in one direction. It helps the reader if this is emphasised by fine rules in one direction only - horizontal rules for tables that are mostly read across, with white space separating the columns.

Tables in which every figure is boxed in, with a grid of both vertical and horizontal rules of the same weight, are daunting to look at and don't help the reader to find his way about.

Some tables contain information that needs to be grouped together. This can be done by introducing either vertical or horizontal rules of a different weight, varying the space between columns or using bold subheadings. Of these the most difficult is the variation in vertical space; if the differences are too subtle they will look like a mistake.

LOA m		Flag
	130 - 160 m	
155.9	Long Lines	USA
150.5	Cable Venture	Great Britain
144.4	Mercury	Great Britain
133.8	Aeolus	USA
130.0	Alert	Great Britain
	100 - 130 m	
119.3	Kuroshio Maru	Japan
115.0	Pacific Guardian	Great Britain
113.8	KDD Maru	Japan
113.2	Cable Enterprise	Great Britain
112.8	Retriever	Great Britain
112.8	Neptune	USA
107.0	Leon Thevenin	France
107.0	Raymond Croze	France
103.5	Salernum	USA
	75 - 100 m	
98.5	Newton	Great Britain
97.2	Monarch	Great Britain

The two boxed tables below cut the information up and drive the reader's eye in the wrong direction.
In the rearranged versions the rules stress the horizontal bias and let the white space provide the vertical divisions.

LOA m		FLAG
	130—160 m	
155.9	Long Lines	USA
150.5	Cable Venture	Great Britain
144.4	Mercury	Great Britain
133.8	Aeolus	USA
130.0	Alert	Great Britain
	100—130 m	
119.3	Kuroshio Maru	Japan
115.0	Pacific Guardian	Great Britain
113.8	KDD Maru	Japan
113.2	Cable Enterprise	Great Britain
112.8	Retriever	Great Britain
112.8	Neptune	USA
107.0	Leon Thevenin	France
107.0	Raymond Croze	France
103.5	Salernum	USA
	75—100 m	
98.5	Newton	Great Britain
97.2	Monarch	Great Britain

TYPE	DATE FIRST USED	MAX FREQ MHz	CIRCUITS		SPACING			LINE CURRENT mA	AMPLIFIERS TYPE
			4 kHz	3 kHz	nm	Cable Size			
						mm	inch		
F60	1956	0.552	60	80	16.5	15.6	0.61	211	Valve
F120	1956	1.164	120		14	16.6	0.65	445	Valve
SD	1966	1.052	96		20	25.4	1.0	325	Valve
S1	1973	1.164	120		17	25.4	1.0	90	Transistor
S5	1970	4.772	480		9	25.4	1.0	180	Transistor

Type for tables

Tables do not have to be in the same typeface as the surrounding text. If, as is often the case, a table contains a lot of numbers then a first consideration must be the clarity of the figures. Sanserif or a conventional roman will normally give a good result although my own preference is for sanserif figures. It is a mistake to use an exotic font with figures that are in any way confusing.

62 135 383 964 172 908

62 135 383 964 172 908

62 135 383 964 172 908

`62 135 383 964 172 908`

The examples above are in the same type size, 10pt. Not only are the first two rows, Times and Helvetica, more legible but they are also the narrowest which means that you can get more information into the table.

Column headings

At the top of each column in a table there will be an identifying heading. These headings should be clearly different from the text and figures in the body of the table and well separated from each other.

- Use as few words as possible:

  weight empty *rather than* weight when empty

  arrives *rather than* time of arrival

- Use bold but keep to upper and lower case.
- If some of the headings run to more than one line then let them hang from the top, don't try to centre them horizontally on each other.
- Put secondary information into a lighter weight on its own line.

weight empty	**height**	**price**
kg	cm	£

- Ranging headings left is simpler but centring them makes the most of the space to keep them apart.

Column widths

The width of each column will depend on the amount of information to be included and the space available. One line for each entry is an ideal but it may be necessary to double up in some columns to get everything into the width. This will of course mean an increase in depth.

Try to keep the table vertical. It is very irritating to have to turn the page through 90 degrees every time the reader wants to refer to a table.

Avoid letting a small amount of a table run over onto the next page. This again is tiresome for the reader and uneconomical as the headings will have to be repeated.

In the case of a very wide table you can use the double spread (two facing pages) but make sure that the break between the pages comes in a sensible place and that the binding method that is to be used is capable of keeping the horizontal alignment.

type	**date first used**	**Max freq**	CIRCUITS		SPACING	**cable size**		**line current**	**amplifiers**
		MHz	4kHz	3kHz	mm	mm	inch	mA	type
F60	1956	0.552	60	80	16.5	15.6	0.61	211	valve
F120	1956	1.164	120		14	16.6	0.65	445	valve
SD	1966	1.052	96		20	25.4	1.0	325	valve
S1	1973	1.164	120		17	25.4	1.0	90	transistor
S5	1970	4.772	480		9	25.4	1.0	180	transistor

Footnotes to tables

Tables can, like diagrams, be something of a blunt instrument. In spite of the impressive array of figures something will have to be left out or certain facts to be inferred from them spelt out to the reader. The usual editorial solution to this problem is to add footnotes to the tables. In academic or scholarly works this is acceptable but for more popular publications they can be distracting and confusing.

However if footnotes have to be included they should be as legible as possible without being intrusive.

In the example below the footnotes are spread across the width of the table...

- Set them in one or two sizes smaller than the text.
- Keep the line lengths to a readable width. Do not spread them out to the full width of the table but set them in two or three columns under the table.
- Make sure that the references to the footnotes in the table cannot be confused with the figures in the body of the table. If there are only one or two footnotes then conventional signs can be used (● + etc). If superior figures are available to you, use them, but if they have been digitised for low resolution they may not be very legible.

Another method, illustrated in the example below, is to use the same figures as in the table but enclosed in square brackets, 138 [1]. This will be clearer but it takes up more space.

Positioning tables

For layout purposes tables can be treated as another variety of illustration and similar considerations apply to their position on the page.

Because they contain text and figures, tables may need to be separated more clearly from the surrounding text than line illustrations or photographs. The simplest way is to put a medium-weight horizontal rule between the table and the adjacent text. Use the same weight of rule each time.

Sun Life	0272-426911	500	250,000	growth	B	3-15	-	6-6.8 [2]	yes
Target	01-2420777	1000	none	both	A	3	Y	7	no
Tyndall	0272-32241	1000	50,000	income	D	3	H	7-7.5[4]	no
		1000	50,000	income	B	5,10	H	6.9-8.[17]	

[1] Returns offered change frequently. Do not choose this column when choosing a bond.
[2] For criteria see box on Company Safety.
[3] Will not work out what you will get from a bond after tax if you do not pay tax at the basic rate only.
[4] Return depends on age and sex.
[5] Technically, a single-premium whole life policy with guaranteed bonuses for period of bond. At end of period, policy has a guaranteed cash-in value.
[6] A friendly society.
[7] Can invest less than £500.
[8] Amount to be paid out by bond, plus life insurance cover from any other life insurance policy, must not exceed £10,000.
[9] Higher rate tax payers can opt for yearly income of five per cent and leave the rest of the return to accumulate until bond ends. This means no tax to pay until the bond ends.

...they are easier to read and take up less space in three columns.

[1] Returns offered change frequently. Do not choose this column when choosing a bond.
[2] For criteria see box on Company Safety.
[3] Will not work out what you will get from a bond after tax if you do not pay tax at the basic rate only.
[4] Return depends on age and sex.
[5] Technically, a single-premium whole life policy with guaranteed bonuses for period of bond. At end of period, policy has a guaranteed cash-in value.
[6] A friendly society.
[7] Can invest less than £500.
[8] Amount to be paid out by bond, plus life insurance cover from any other life insurance policy, must not exceed £10,000.
[9] Higher rate tax payers can opt for yearly income of five per cent and leave the rest of the return to accumulate until bond ends. This means no tax to pay until the bond ends.

Tables often give statistical support to the accompanying text or provide information from which the reader is intended to draw conclusions. If the reader is unlikely to have time to look too closely, it can be helpful to spell out the features which are considered editorially important. In this way the tables actively support the editorial rather than appearing as a daunting row of figures.

In the example below, the strong divisions between the main groups and the generous space between the lines make more rules unnecessary. The panels at the side make the important points for the casual reader. The more tenacious can still go into the detailed figures if they want to.

A table intended for experts but made easier to use by careful layout and organisation. (reduced)

Invisible earnings of UK banking sector — Table 24

£ million		1970	1971	1972	1973	1974	1975	1976
Credits	Financial and allied services	48	59	78	92	109	127	169
	Interest and discount on export credit	60	68	77	105	132	147	172
	Investment income from and services rendered to overseas branches etc	60	58	85	123	104	129	145
	Interest and discount on other lending in sterling	53	38	54	98	141	168	211
	Net interest on borrowing and lending in overseas currencies	16	16	44	18	16	158	266
	Total	**237**	**239**	**338**	**436**	**502**	**729**	**963**
Debits	Investment income due to and services rendered by overseas branches etc	37	58	82	97	142	194	257
	Interest on borrowing in sterling	97	98	126	222	325	331	298
	Total	**134**	**156**	**208**	**319**	**467**	**525**	**555**
Net earnings		**103**	**83**	**130**	**117**	**35**	**204**	**408**

Vices

	price £	fixing	jaw width mm	max opening mm	throat depth mm	comments
WOODWORKING (or carpenters)						
Robin Goodmann	8.13	screws	150	125	50	satisfactory
Reechards	37.05	bolts	265	380	105	good
Parana	8.75	screws	150	120	55	well liked by users
Whiteleaf	7.08	screws	155	120	50	could bruise wood
L-SHAPED (or corner)						
Robin Goodmann	8.23	clamp	125	95	40	fixed at right end
Storey	7.45	clamp	125	90	40	fixed at left end
METALWORKING						
Dropper	10.21	bolts	80	75	50	good sturdy vice
Drunford	5.94	clamp	60	50	25	reasonable grip
Fowler	8.51	suction	65	45	30	unstable
Parana	15.39	screws	55	60	30	gripped well

You get what you pay for, the most expensive is the best

Which end will be fixed?

Bolts and screws provide the most stable fixing

Notes

Many texts will have some sort of annotation and their handling will be important to the appearance of the page and the understanding of the text. For the most part, notes either provide cross references or amplify the main text with subsidiary but important information.

Cross references

These can be dealt with either by footnotes on the page or, if there are a lot of them, by grouping them together at the end of the document. Even in academic works constant cross referencing can be an irritation to the reader but in more general publications they are better relegated to a general bibliography at the end.

If footnotes are inevitable then they should be set smaller than the main text, two sizes smaller if that is available. If there are only one or two on the page then use asterisks and other conventional signs (* + #) to refer to them in the text but if there are more than two or three footnotes, figures will have to be used. Superior figures ($^{1\ 2\ 3}$) are the usual convention but text size figures in square brackets can also be used [1]. In any case whatever method is adopted it must be used consistently throughout the document.

There is no need to use superior figures to identify the footnotes themselves but a hanging indent is sometimes helpful. As the text is smaller there will be more characters to the line so if the text measure is too wide the notes can be set to a narrower measure in two columns under the text.

Three ways of marking footnotes

Conventional signs, only suitable if there are very few footnotes on each page. The notes themselves are treated with a hanging indent.

The need for all agencies, local and central, to take full account of local interests was emphasised by section 37 of the 1968 Act.*

During our review we have paid particular attention to the relationship between the purposes of the parks and local interests.+ In this connection we mustdraw attention

* Councils for the protection of Rural England and Wales.

\+ Committee on Land Utilisation in Rural Areas Cmd 6378.

Superior figures within the text and lining figures in the notes. Also with a hanging indent.

The need for all agencies, local and central, to take full account of local interests was emphasised by section 37 of the 1968 Act.^{1}

During our review we have paid particular attention to the relationship between the purposes of the parks and local interests.^{2} In this connection we must draw attention

1 Councils for the protection of Rural England and Wales.

2 Committee on Land Utilisation in Rural Areas Cmd 6378.

Bracketed figures both in the text and in the notes, with no indent.

The need for all agencies, local and central, to take full account of local interests was emphasised by section 37 of the 1968 Act.[1]

During our review we have paid particular attention to the relationship between the purposes of the parks and local interests.[2] In this connection we must draw attention

[1] Councils for the protection of Rural England and Wales.

[2] Committee on Land Utilisation in Rural Areas Cmd 6378.

Annotations

Notes which amplify the text invariably need to be on the same page, or at least the same spread, as the relevant text. These can again be treated as footnotes but more interest and 'colour' can be given to the page if they are incorporated in other ways.

Marginal notes

These usually run in the left-hand margin. They are treated in the same way as side headings and need a similar page layout with a wide side margin to take them. As they are likely to run beyond the main text to which they refer they are best set in a size smaller.

Cut-in notes within the text

These can look decorative and help to break up the text. Like many such devices they can become irritating and distracting if over-used. They are also quite difficult to manage technically and can take a lot of time to insert. In any case they are not suitable for notes of more than a few lines. They look better if the main text is justified.

Small type for devotees

Sometimes the essential message contained in a particular piece of copy gets lost in a mass of background information which may be relevant and necessary to back up the argument but which clouds the one or two points the reader needs to remember. In this event it is better to limit the main text to the salient points you want to make and separate the background information as a long note which the reader can refer to if he wants.

These passages, which can take up a whole column or even half a page, can be set a size smaller than the main copy and boxed off or put under a coloured tint to add interest to the page while the reader can concentrate on the essential message.

Examples of marginal notes and cut-in notes

There are three main retirement pensions from the state: Basic (flat rate) pension; Additional (earnings related); and Graduated pension.
The basic pension is paid to everyone - including married women.

Even if your retirement seems a long way off, what you do now could affect your pension in the future.

Planning for retirement ought to start as early as leaving school. At that age it may seem absurd to worry about what will happen to you at the end of your working life - and many people don't give the matter enough thought until they are well into middle age.

How much State pension you will get will depend on your paying National Insurance contributions over many years.

The standard pension rate is laid down each year by the Government. If you have too few contributions to qualify for the full amount, you might still be able to get a proportion of it.

If you are a member of a 'contracted out' scheme see box.

You can qualify for an additional pension only for periods spent working for an employer. You cannot contribute to the additional pension scheme while you are self-employed or not working. The amount you get depends on your earnings and how many years you have contributed. Graduated pensions are a relic of the state scheme which existed from 1961 to 1975. They were a simpler version of today's additional pension scheme but the amounts paid out are small.

For Retail Price Index see page 32.

State pensions may not seem very large compared with your earnings, but they are a valuable source of retirement income because they are 'inflation proofed'. They are increased each November by the change in the Retail Price Index over the 12 months to the preceding May. There are also non-contributory pensions available to retired people mainly on low incomes.

Illustration

A picture might just be worth a thousand words but don't expect your readers always to know what they should be.

Line and tone

Illustrations can be either *line* or *halftone*.

Line illustrations are made up of solid lines or black areas without any gradations from one grey area to another. Grey areas can be added by the use of tints which themselves consist of black dots, lines or other patterns. Because, like the surrounding type, line illustrations are made up of clear black lines, they can be photographed for reproduction onto a printing plate at the same time as the text.

Line subject.

Halftones can reproduce fine gradations from one grey tone to another, sometimes referred to as 'continuous tone'. All photographic illustration has to be reproduced by some form of halftone process, either by rephotographing the original through a screen or by electronic scanning. Any drawn illustration which includes subtle grey washes also has to be treated as a halftone.

While it is necessary to understand the technical difference between line and tone it is more important to be able to decide when to use drawn illustration or photographs.

A continuous tone photograph with, below, an enlarged detail showing how it is broken up into dots by the halftone screen.

Drawn illustration

Drawings include both pictorial illustrations and diagrams. In either case they have to be generated by an artist, draughtsman or a fairly sophisticated drawing programme on the word processor. The advantage of drawn illustration is that it can be directed to contain any images you want so that particular points can be emphasised or special features highlighted. They can sometimes be used more freely than photographs within the text which makes them useful for relieving long text passages.

However if drawings are to be effective and convincing they have to be done well. This often means employing a professional. It is very tempting to save money on illustration by employing amateurs or inexperienced students. Of course they may be very gifted and the result a success, but it is more likely that the quality of the illustration will not match up to the rest of the production. If a lot of time and money has been spent on preparing the document it is foolish to spoil it with weak illustration.

If a drawing needs correcting **never mark the original.** Always indicate the corrections on a transparent overlay or make a copy and make the corrections on that.

Cartoons
Funny drawings have a place in many documents but they are frequently over-used partly because they are the first idea anybody has and partly because nobody can think of any other way of breaking up the text.

A really good cartoon can enliven and comment on the text. The best ideas are usually the ones that come from the cartoonists themselves rather than those which are just an amusing drawing of someone else's idea of a joke. Give the cartoonist the text and let him have his own ideas. If he is any good he will see things in it that will be a surprise to those who have been working on it.

Charts and diagrams

Besides giving information in a graphic form, charts and diagrams can provide visual interest but it is important that these two aims are not allowed to conflict. Charts can be made more interesting by drawing them in perspective or by adding shading and tints. But these must be done in a way that augments the message rather than confuses it.

Diagrams can be an invaluable aid in supplying supporting evidence in a document and as a way of getting a lot of information into a small space which would otherwise have to be spelt out in the text, but do not assume that the reader is going to see in a diagram what you want or expect him to see.

Diagrams are for the most part a blunt instrument and are best used to show trends and very broad movements. If a document is aimed at an academic audience it is probably safe to assume that they will understand whatever diagrams are included but for more popular publications it can help the reader's understanding if the diagrams are well labelled and the significance of the statistics emphasised.

If when you have drawn a diagram you feel obliged to support it with endless footnotes, ask yourself whether a diagram is the best answer to the problem.

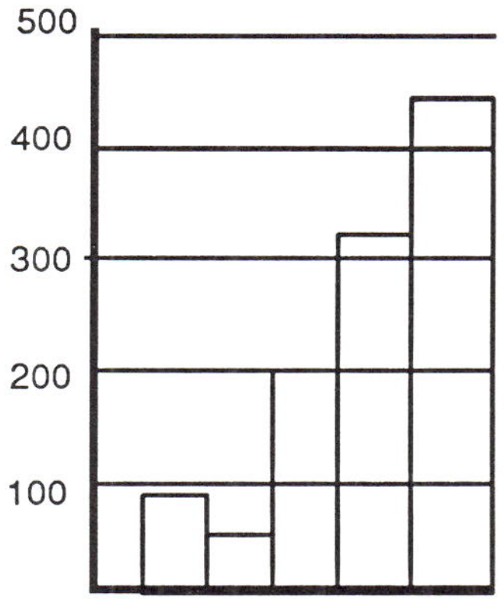

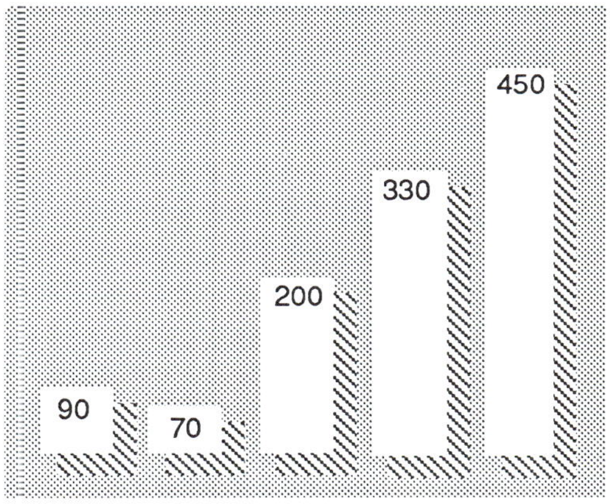

Quite a small amount of graphic shadow effect adds life to a simple bar chart, but it is the extra figures that add to its usefulness.

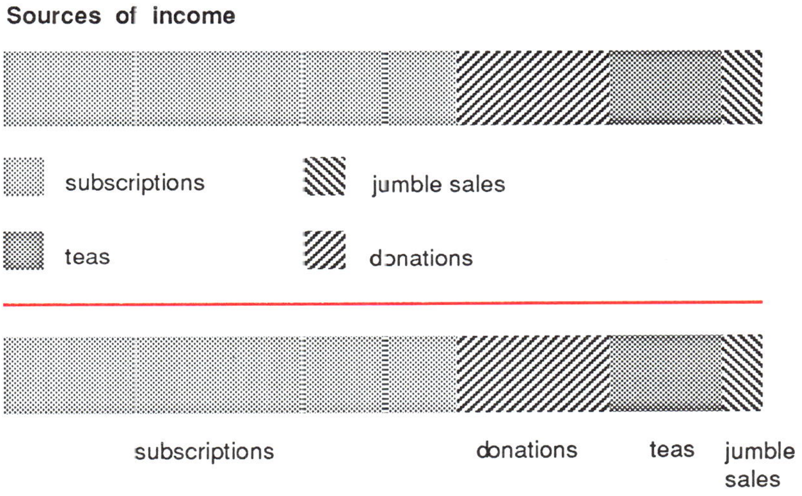

Beware of 'keys' to diagrams. In the simple example above the addition of a key makes it more difficult to extract the information. The lower version is easier to read.

Keep the background grids to graphs as simple as possible but sufficient to make the meaning clear.

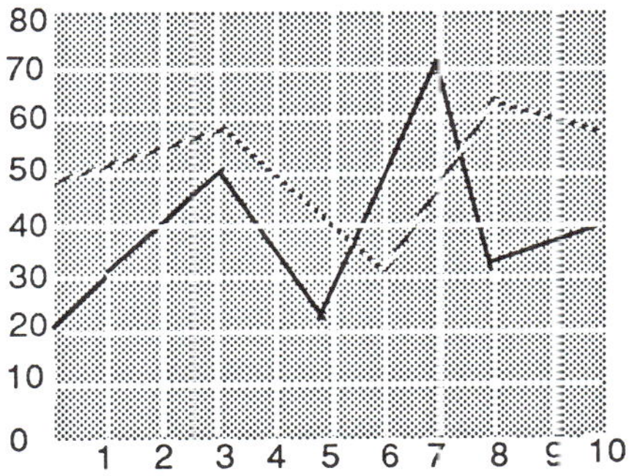

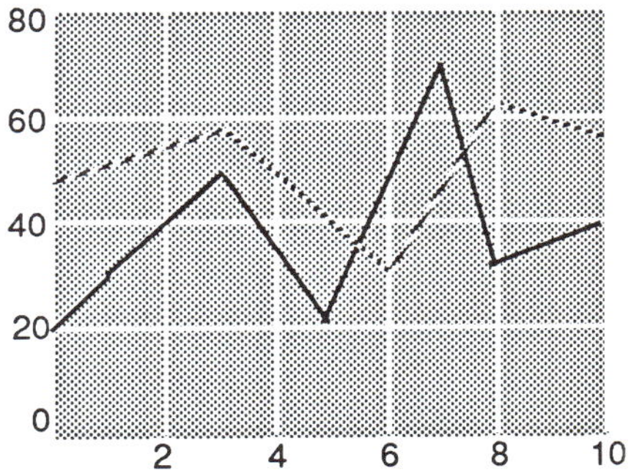

Pies, bars and graphs
These are the three most popular ways of presenting statistical information in graphic form. Their frequent use does not mean that they are as easy to plan as they look nor may they necessarily be the best type of diagram for the information you want to convey.

Before planning any diagram check:

The gap between the biggest and the smallest figures to be represented.

The varieties of scale you are being asked to use.

How many different pieces of information you are expecting to get onto one diagram.

A big gap between the highest and lowest figures can present problems, particularly in bar and pie charts. It will almost certainly mean that, unless the diagram occupies a lot of space, the scale will have to be so fine that it will be very difficult to see the difference between one figure and another (*seeing* the difference is the point of diagrams). It will also be impossible to show the smallest numbers accurately. One solution may be to add the figures, as numerals, to each bar or section of the pie rather than relying on a scale. Adding the figures to the diagram is often helpful, even when the scale is quite large.

Varieties of scale should be avoided, particularly if information in different charts is to be compared.

Too many different pieces of information in one diagram is likely to be confusing. If the figures can be separated it is usually better to have two small charts than one big one that is overloaded.

In graphs, the narrower the scale along the bottom axis the more dramatic will be the difference between one figure and another. Always keep the grid lines to a minimum.

Graphics do not have to be limited to charts and graphs. Decorative elements can be created on a PC, but they take time and care. They will always look slightly mechanical but this can be relieved by removing the hard key line edges.

Design by Rachel Beckley

Photographic illustration

Readers tend to think of photographs as being more 'real' than drawings, and indeed a good photograph can carry a great deal of conviction. But as with drawings much depends on the quality of the original. A publication illustrated entirely with the managing director's snap shots is unlikely either to be compelling or look well produced.

One of the problems for in-house publications is the subject matter of photographs. If a photograph is not taken specially to illustrate a particular subject, it is almost certain to miss out some vital detail. In the end it is usually quicker and more satisfactory to commission at least some photographs for the more important subjects.

This includes portrait photographs or 'mug shots'. Huge international companies will spend a great deal of money on their annual report but still 'economise' by using a random collection of photographs of their company directors, all at different scales and with different backgrounds.

Too many 'mug shots' can kill a publication. The inevitable political pressures to include Mr A because Mr B is on the previous page should be resisted.

Squared up or cut out
Photographs which are a simple rectangle are referred to as 'squared up', while photographs from which some or all of the background has been removed are called 'cut outs'. Cutting out must be done by a skilled hand. A badly made cut out with odd bumps on it does no credit to a publication.

There are no rules for when to use one or the other. A well made cut out can be dramatic and add life to a page, but the original must be suited to the treatment. The cut out shape must be clearly defined against the background.

Too detailed a subject, for example a wire basket, can be difficult to define and may break down. Make sure that there are no extraneous bits of the picture coming across the cut out subject, like somebody's hand or foot.

Bled photographs
When a photograph, tint panel or any other illustration runs off the edge of the page it is said to 'bleed'. In order to achieve this in printing the illustration has to be scaled to allow an extra 1/8" or 4mm on the bled side(s). This is to compensate for any movement in the paper during printing and to allow for the tolerances needed in trimming the paper.

The width does not have to be increased where the picture runs into the back of the page but remember that, with some methods of binding, it is possible to lose some of the picture into the back.

The effect of bleeding on the layout is to give a very powerful direction to the page. Full page bleeds can be spectacular and useful as section dividers, but don't forget that you may have to make room for a caption on the opposite page.

It is particularly important to plan pages with bled pictures as spreads. The direction of the bleeds will profoundly affect the appearance of the opposite page.

Make sure that the direction of the bled photographs compliment one another rather than conflict. Bleed in corners (top or foot and back or foredge) can stop the flow of pages with an otherwise strong horizontal or vertical thrust. It is perfectly possible to mix bled and unbled pictures on the same spread but be careful of awkward conjunctions giving uncomfortable areas of white margin.

Full page bleed.

The bleeds in this spread reinforce the layout of the pages.

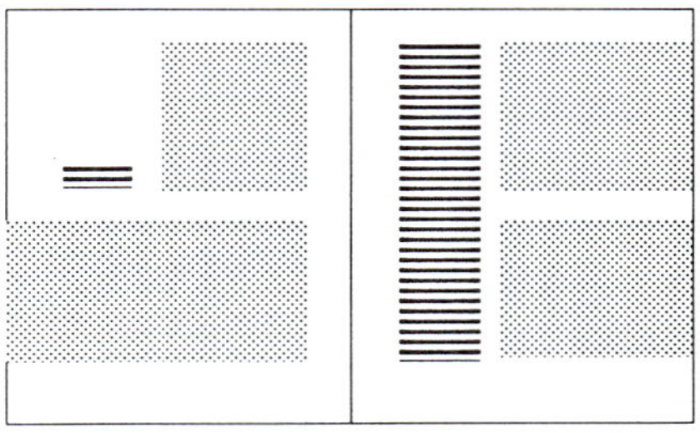

The bleed at the bottom corner breaks up the layout.

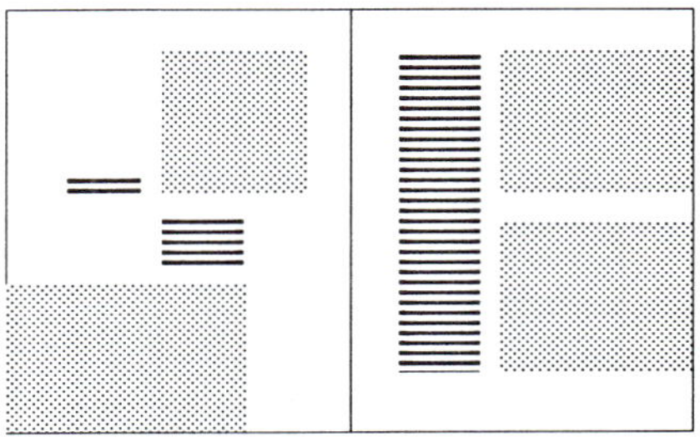

Bleeds top and right.

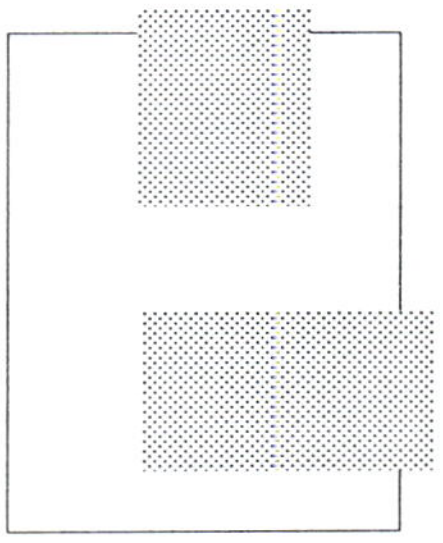

Random bleeds make for an ugly spread.

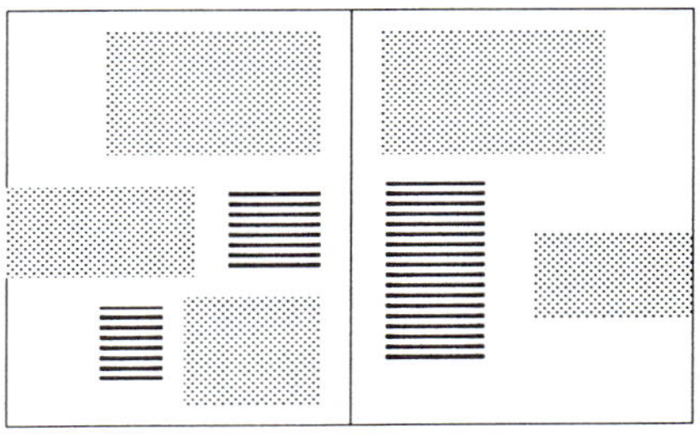

Cropping photographs either to fit the space available or to remove unwanted background is a skilled business. Assuming that the picture has a particular story to tell, then whatever cropping has to be done must preserve that central message. Look at the background and decide if it is important to the picture as a whole or whether it is in fact distracting. Try masking the background with white paper to see what happens when it is cropped and to decide on the best composition.

Portraits need particular care; if you decide that you don't want yards of dark suit, crop right up to the shoulders, not half-way through the hands, and watch out for that pocket handkerchief making a little white triangle at the bottom of the picture.

As a general rule it is better to have one good picture, big, than four small ones. Remember that your readers will not know what you have left out and if they are hurriedly skimming through the publication their attention is more likely to be arrested by the one big photograph. If there are a number of small pictures, group them together rather than distribute them in unrelated positions on the page.

Photomontage or collage of photographs or newspaper headlines is, like cartoons, often a solution of first resort. In fact it should be the very last hope when every other more imaginative avenue has been exhausted. Its use usually means that nobody can decide what is the most important issue and so a compromise is struck by trying to get everything into the act. Good montage can be effective but mostly it looks tired and overworked.

Scaling photographs

In order to plan a layout which includes illustrations it will be necessary to know exactly how much space they are going to occupy or how much they will have to be cropped to fit the space available.

To find the height of a rectangular illustration if it is reduced to a given width (*x*).

Take a piece of transparent paper big enough to cover the original.

Draw a right-angle 2 or 3 cms in from the left-hand edge of the paper and the bottom of the sheet (AB BC).

Measure the given width (*x*) along the bottom line (BC) and draw a vertical line from that point (DE).

Lay the paper over the illustration with the lines AB and BC on the left-hand and bottom edges of the original.

Draw a diagonal from the corner B through the top right-hand corner of the illustration (BF).

The point at which the diagonal BF crosses the vertical DE is the height that the illustration will make if it is reduced to *x* wide.

If the illustration is irregular in shape, draw a rectangle (on an overlay sheet, not on the original) round the extremities of the image and scale it in the same way.

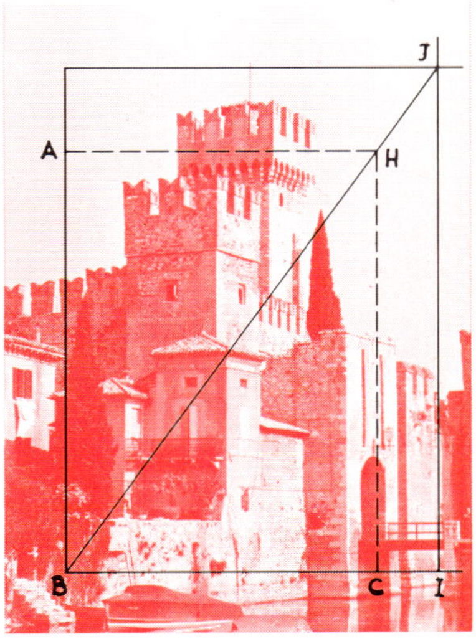

To scale and crop an illustration to fit a given area, the same principle applies.

Draw the area to be filled (dotted line) in the corner of the right-angle.

Draw a diagonal from corner to corner (BH) and extend it beyond the rectangle.

Lay it over the part of the picture you want to include. Select the widest point on the right of the picture and draw a vertical (IJ) from the base BC.

The point where that line crosses the diagonal marks the level at which the picture will have to be cropped to fit the given area when reduced (or enlarged).

If too much is being cropped from the top and you cannot take any more off the bottom then you will have to use more of the picture's limits to the right or left.

Captions for illustrations

Fitting captions is part of the design problem. Readers should not be left in any doubt about which illustration is which. Nor should they be compelled to play 'hunt the caption'.

The treatment of the captions will depend on the nature of the illustrations and their relation to the text. In rare cases, when illustrations are purely decorative, captions may not be necessary, although the reader may be glad of a list of them somewhere in the document. For the most part illustrations do need captions and it is important for the reader that they are positioned intelligently and helpfully.

Type for captions
Captions need to be distinguished from the text. The simplest way to achieve the difference is to set them a size smaller. However this can look ugly and make them too small for comfort - particularly in low resolution.

Alternatives include:

- Setting in the same size as the text but in a different weight or style (bold, light, italic or a different type face).
- If colour is available, setting them to the text size and weight but printing them in colour.
- Setting in the same size as the text but neatly and consistently ruling them off to link them to the illustration.

Much will depend on how important the captions are to the rest of the text. If they are merely identifying illustrations with a number and a short title, then a smaller size is probably the best solution. But if they are extended captions to be read in their own right apart from the text, then one of the other methods might be considered.

Positioning captions
The obvious position for captions is at a constant distance below the relevant illustration and for many documents this will be the best solution. But captions can be a moveable element which can help to enliven a page or, unless sensitively placed, they can interfere with an otherwise neat and stylish layout.

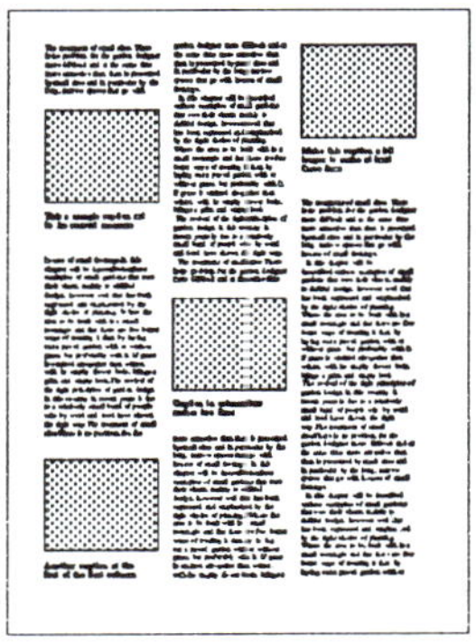

Simple but dull.

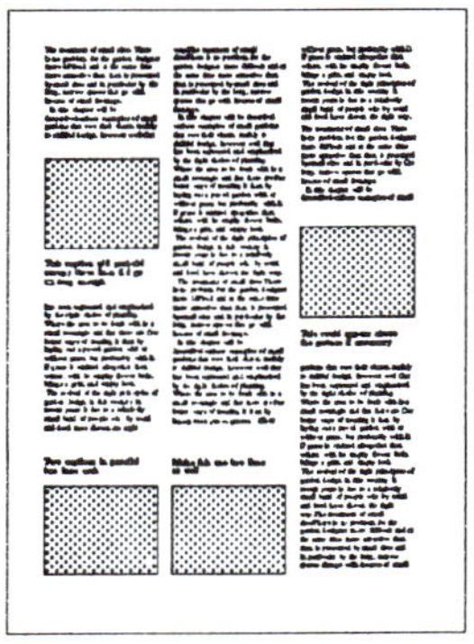

Makes a nice, clean line at the foot of the page but inconsistent position could be confusing.

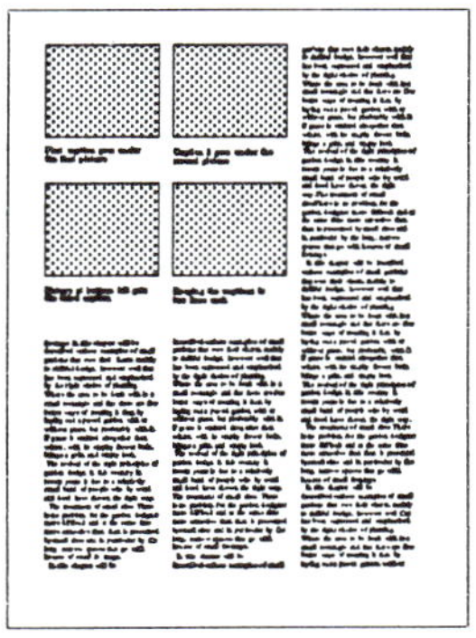

Grouping small pictures together helps with captioning.

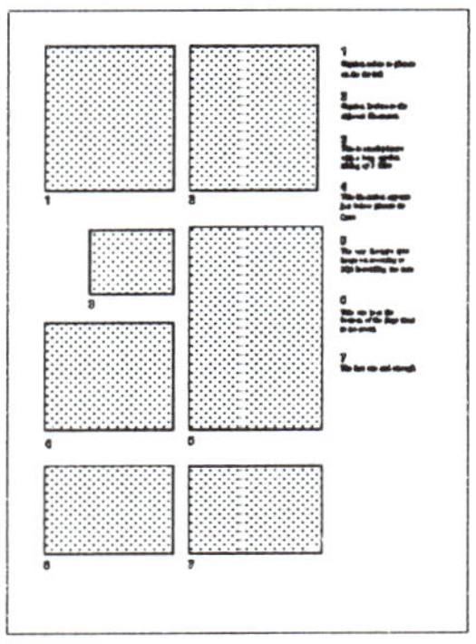

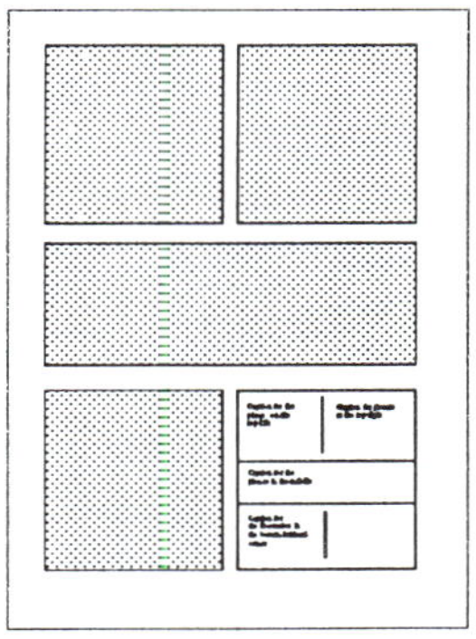

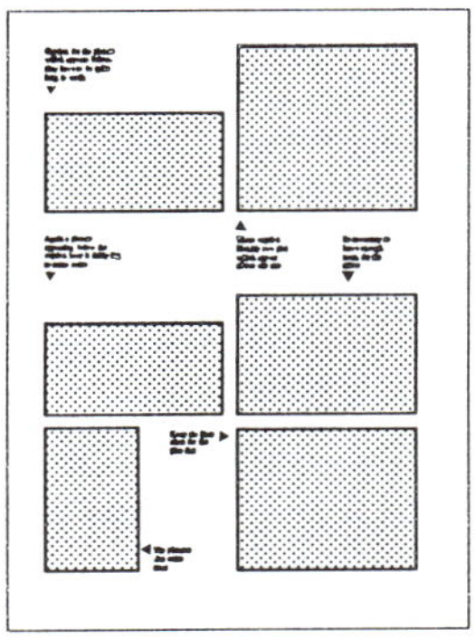

Other caption arrangements
These methods are all best suited to pages in which illustrations predominate. They have the disadvantage that the reader has to look carefully to be sure which caption belongs to which picture. The advantage is that the captions do not interfere with or dominate the illustrations.

Cover design

The cover should reflect the style of the rest of the document. But just as the cover paper works better if it is stiffer than the text paper so the treatment of the cover should be stronger than the typography of the inside.

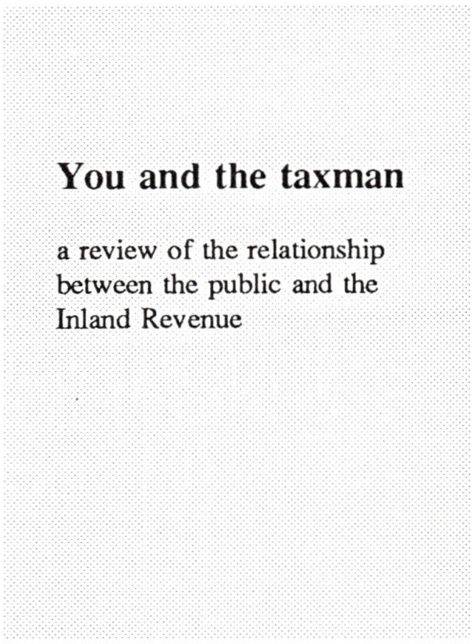

The design of a cover will depend on the job it has to do. If it has to provide merely a protective wrapping and identify the contents then a neatly arranged bold title on a semi-stiff board may be enough.

Quite simple typography has more chance of getting the casual reader to look twice than either undue modesty or too much decoration.

If the publication has to gain the attention of the reader on its way from the envelope to the waste-paper basket then something a good deal more forceful is needed. If the message is strong and simple then the best solution may well be good, clear typography. Illustrations can help but only if they are relevant and good quality. A murky snapshot or crude cartoon is unlikely to win hearts and minds.

The cover has to catch the eye and say something about the contents so that the reader is persuaded to open it and read on. The cover should not be something that readers have to pore over to understand but rather it has to be the vehicle for an immediate and easily assimilated message.

If the cover is to have a graphic image there should be one image only. Do not be tempted to illustrate every subject that appears in the publication. By the time readers have worked out what it all means they will have lost interest and passed on to something else. The illustration can always be supported with a list of the most important features.

The single-image formula for almost all magazines that appear on bookstalls. Designing a cover which has to compete on a bookstall is a very skilled business which is usually best left to the professional.

Standard covers

It is sometimes convenient to have a standard cover which can be used to contain different but similar documents. The usual method is to pre-print the cover board with standard information such as the company name and address. The cover has a window cut in it which reveals the name of the document printed on the title page. This is adequate for simple, prosaic documents but the result is likely to be uninspiring. A lot of the trouble that has been taken to make a more interesting job of the text pages will be wasted if too many short cuts are taken with the cover.

A standard layout can be prepared giving the position and specification of the constant information which appears on the cover and a position designated for the title, author, number or any other variable details. This allows more information to appear on the cover than can be seen through a window and permits the typography of the cover to be more forceful than that of the title page. If the cover is produced on a laser printer or copier it can be reproduced on any colour paper or thin card.

The standard cover, with a window revealing the title on the first page, is convenient but limits the impact.

Overprinting the title is not as expensive as it used to be and gives more opportunity to make a strong cover.

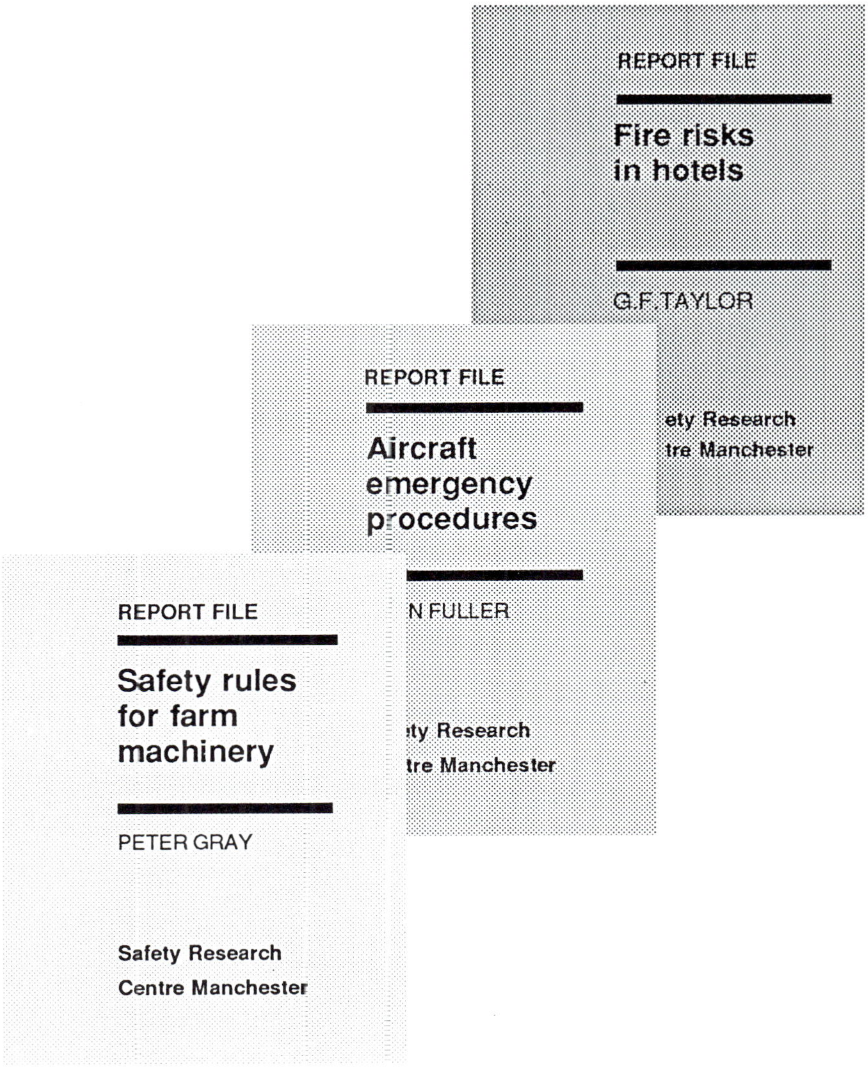

Tabloid mastheads

The title has to be powerful enough to hold its own on a varied page. On the other hand the title will be repeated on each issue, so readers will be used to it and identify the publication by the 'image' created by the title as much as by the name itself.

The name of the publication should be clear and strong but not so overpowering as to dominate the most important news headlines. It helps if it appears in a constant position on the sheet each time. Reversing the lettering out of a colour panel can give extra power to a relatively modest title.

The styles of lettering available on your personal computer may not be ideal for banner titling. As the lettering will be used many times it may be worth investing in a piece of professionally drawn lettering or type setting.

There will also be other important information, such as the date and issue number, which should appear in a constant position together with the title lettering so that readers know where to find it.

A masthead made on a PC (top) may be too limiting. Drawn or dry-transfer lettering can give more variety, particularly if you have the facility to scan or digitise it onto a disc.

Reversing out of a solid gives more impact to a smaller heading.

If the cover does not have to compete on a bookstall; running the title down the side leaves the full page depth to display the text.

Colour

If a document is to be printed by offset then colour can be used. For most in-house documents the use of colour will be limited to one or two used within the text.

Hue and tone

When considering colour in print it is important to distinguish between hue and tone. Hue is what is usually refered to as the colour of a pigment - red, blue, orange etc. Tone refers to its brightness from dark to light. The choice of hue is often very subjective. The tonal characteristics however have practical considerations which must be borne in mind when choosing a colour.

Very dark tones - deep blues, reds and greens - will read clearly if they are used for text on white paper but they will not contrast well with black and so may not stand out from the surrounding black text if they are used for emphasis. Neither will black text be very readable if it is printed over a dark colour which is itself approaching black. Conversely dark tones make an excellent background for white lettering reversed out of a solid colour.

Light tones - pale pinks or yellows - will make a good background for dark lettering but any text printed in such a tone on white paper is likely to disappear. Similarly white lettering on a pale background will not read well.

While this is a matter of common sense it does mean that it is important to plan in advance exactly how you are going to use colour before deciding on a particular shade of ink.

Some colours are always fairly safe. Bright reds, blues and tan browns will make a good background to either black or white text and will be readable if used for the type itself.

Bright greens or orange usually work well as background colours but tend to weaken noticeably when used for type on white paper unless they are carefully selected. Yellow is suitable only as a background colour.

Colour and monochrome copiers

If a document is to be copied in black and white, then not only will the effect of colour in the original be lost but some colours may not print at all.

As a general rule the paler colours, particularly in the blue part of the spectrum, will tend to disappear while the stronger colours, especially if they contain red, will reproduce well in black. But a red background overprinted with black type will copy as a black solid and the type will disappear completely.

Using colour for emphasis

The same principles apply to the use of colour for emphasis as to the use of bold type. Use it discriminately and consistently.

Colour can be used in the hierarchy of subheadings. It may not necessarily make a heading more prominent - just different. The weight of the type and the space round it will also have an important part to play.

Coloured rules can be very effective but again the same principles apply as for black rules.

Coloured panels can be used instead of boxes to separate text. A solid panel may dominate the page. A tint of the colour will often be enough although a colour which looks very attractive printed as a solid may be disappointing as a tint. This applies particularly to very dark tones which tend to look rather grey when broken up into dots.

Using two colours without black

If two colours are available it is not always necessary for one of them to be black.

If the document is fairly short without very long passages of text - a four-page leaflet for example - it can be made more lively and attractive by using two colours other than black. The colours will have to be carefully selected to ensure that their tone is dark enough to read well and sufficiently different to be effective. This device does not usually work well for very long texts.

If flat areas are being used, the two colours can be overprinted to give a third, eg blue and red giving purple. Do not ask the printer to overprint small areas such as fine rules or type.

Bear in mind how the document will be used. If it is to be read in a yellow, artificial light then colours in that part of the spectrum will be absorbed and not read well. Choosing a colour other than black for reproducing halftone illustrations calls for skill and experience. If you are not confident don't risk it.

Binding

The method, style and quality of binding will not improve a poorly laid out document but a bad or inappropriate binding can ruin a good layout.

The type of binding will depend on what is available, the method of printing and the way in which the document is to be used.

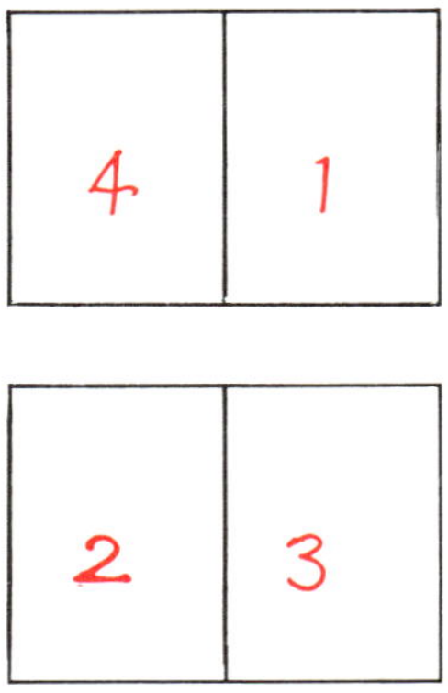

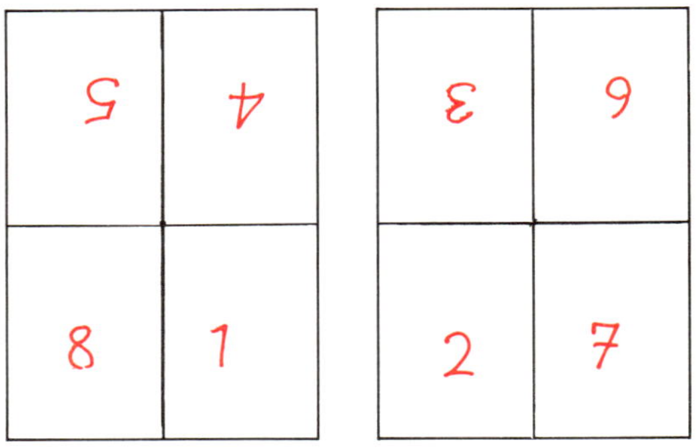

How the pages fall.
Left: 4-page section
Above: 8-page section

Binding folded sheets

If a document is printed so that pairs of pages are printed together on the same sheet they can be stitched or wire stapled together through the fold. This is called saddle-stitching.

This is a familiar method used by printers who will have the necessary equipment to do it accurately and efficiently.

Each folded sheet carries at least four pages - two front and two back - so all saddle-stitched documents have to be made up of multiples of four pages (8,12,16,20...). You can't have a six-page document saddle-stitched. Most printers prefer to work in multiples of at least eight pages. This is not as limiting as it sounds. There are plenty of ways of absorbing an extra page - by having a separate contents page, starting sections on a new page or even a right-hand page and of course leaving the last page blank. Or if for instance you have run over onto page 9 by only a few lines, a bit of judicious cutting can save a complete four-page section.

Providing that the paper is not too heavy, documents of up to 32 pages can be saddle-stitched in one section. Much more than that and you begin to get an unsightly swelling at the fold and the document may not close well.

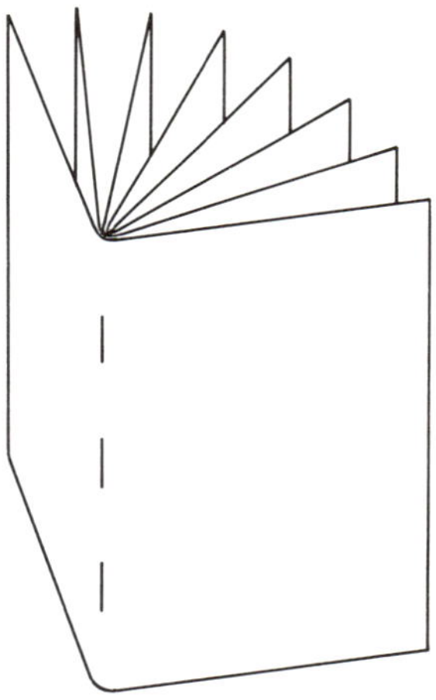

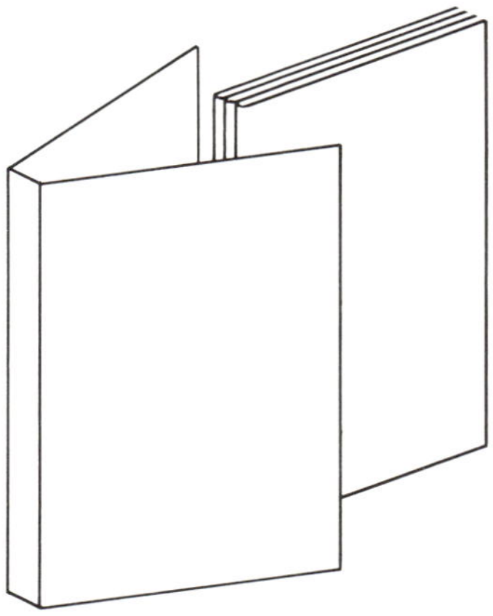

More than 48 pages and you will have to bind in more than one section and draw the cover round it or consider one of the other methods available.

In any case saddle-stitched binding needs professional skills and equipment. Its advantage is that it is neat and reliable.

If it is intended to have saddle-stitched something that is going to be printed in-house, particularly if it is more than 16 pages, it is wise to get professional advice first. In order to keep the folded document to a consistent size, the outside sheet of a 32-page section will in fact be slightly bigger than the inside four-page sheet. This has to be allowed for in the makeup of the pages for the printer.

Left: a 16-page section, saddle-stitched and several sections with a drawn-on cover.

Binding single sheets

Side stabbing
Wire staples are driven through the sides of the sheets on the left-hand edge. This can include the cover sheet or a folded cover can be drawn round afterwards.

Advantages: cheap and relatively easy to do. A few pages can even be stabbed with an office stapler.

Disadvantages: a crude and clumsy method which does not allow the document to open easily or stay open. Pages cannot be added after binding. Use only as a last resort.

Remember: allow a very big back margin, at least 4cm,or the text will get lost in the backs.

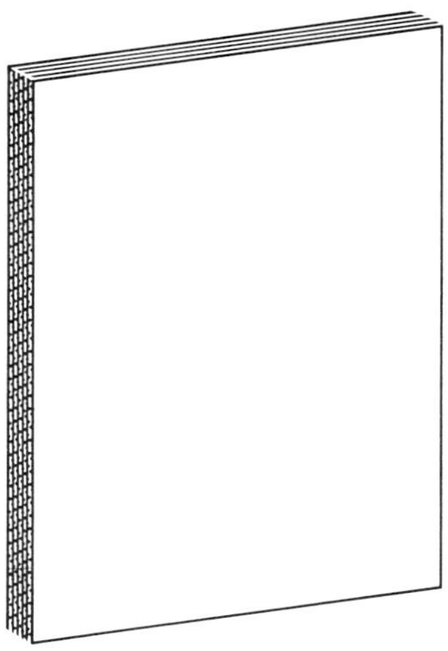

Perfect binding
The single sheets are clamped tightly together and a thin layer of plastic glue is applied along the spine. When this method was first introduced in the 1950s there were some disasters and even today a faulty copy can fall to bits. But on the whole it works well and is widely used for anything from telephone directories to books and annual reports.

Advantages: neat and if well done allows the pages to open easily. Need not be expensive. Some manufacturers make desk models which work well.

Disadvantages: only suitable for fairly thick documents which have enough pages to allow the glue to hold. Not suitable for anything less than 32 pages and even then better done professionally. Pages cannot be added after binding. Works and looks best with a four-page cover wrapped round it.

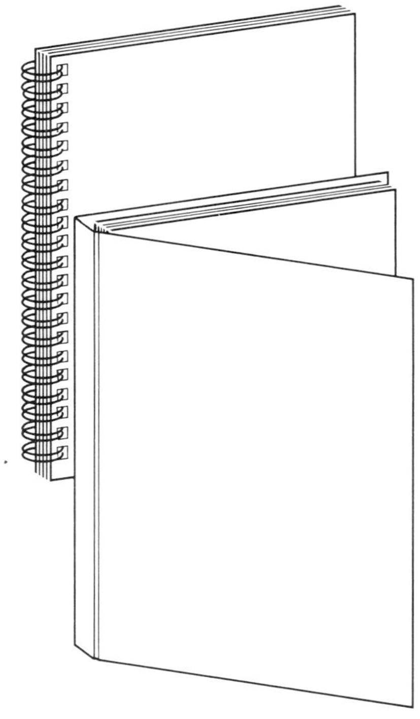

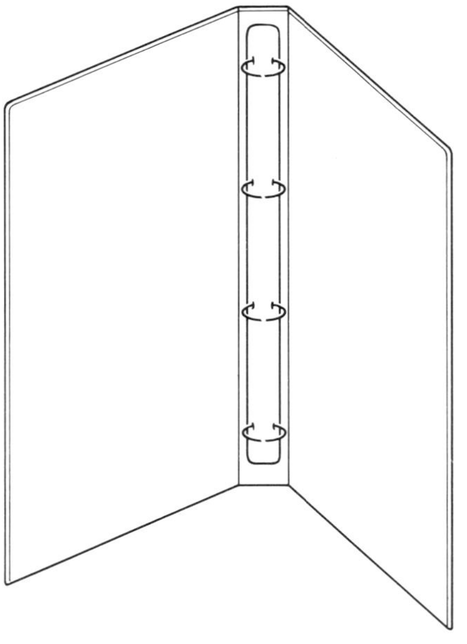

Wire or plastic binding
Holes are punched along the left-hand edge of the sheets and a patent wire or plastic clasp is meshed into the holes.

Advantages: the necessary equipment is relatively cheap and can be used by any neat-fingered operator in an office. Different diameters of coil allow almost any number of pages to be bound. Documents open flat. A cheap way of getting a neat result.

Disadvantages: documents bound in this way are not always easy to store. The wires, which are wider than the publication, can be tiresome on a bookshelf and a number of them side by side can get inextricably entwined. This problem can be avoided by wrapping a cover round the document, concealing the wires.

Remember: allow enough margin for the holes to be punched without cutting into the text.

Ring binders
Two or four holes are punched on the left-hand edge and the sheets threaded onto fittings in the binder.

Advantages: simple and cheap. Ready-made binders, which are easy to get, can be silk screened with a special title if needed. Pages can be added or taken out easily. Particularly good for any document that needs constant updating. Pages will always lie flat and stay open.

Disadvantages: if heavily used, pages can wear at the holes unless reinforced. Can be very tiresome to store as the spine is invariably wider than the foredge. If the publication is slim, the binding can overpower the contents.

Remember: if they have to be sent through the post they may need special packing. Leave enough back margin to allow for the holes which may come in further than in wire binding.

Plastic grip binders
A plastic strip is slid along the spine tightly gripping the pages.

Advantages: simple and very cheap. Strips in various colours can be bought from most big stationers. Requires little skill once you have got the knack. Pages can be added or removed.

Disadvantages: pages do not open easily and never flat. If an impatient reader tries to force the pages back they can spring out with some force. Not suited to any document that is going to get a lot of use.

Remember: leave an extra big margin in the back, at least 4cm. It helps if the cover board is scored along the folding edge, against the plastic strip.

Some useful folds

Documents occupying only one or two sheets can be folded in a number of ways which can help to divide the text and add interest.

A3 folded once
Four pages (A4) 210 x 297mm

A4 folded once across
Four pages (A5) 148 x 210mm

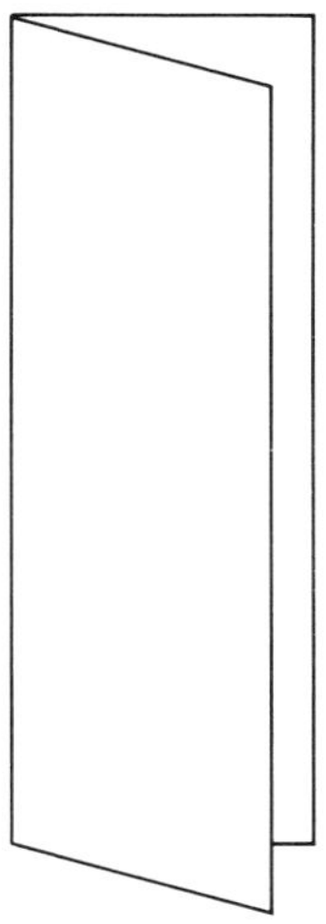

A4 folded once lengthways
Four pages 105 x 297
This gives a very tall, narrow format. Occasionally useful for leaflets to be inserted into another A4 document.

A4 folded twice (gate fold)
Six pages 99 x 210mm - fits standard DL envelope, (see *Paper*).
Remember that the leaf that folds inside should be slightly narrower (4mm or 1/8") than the other two leaves, otherwise the document might not lay flat when folded.

A4 folded twice (concertina fold)
Six pages 99 x 210mm - fits standard DL envelope.

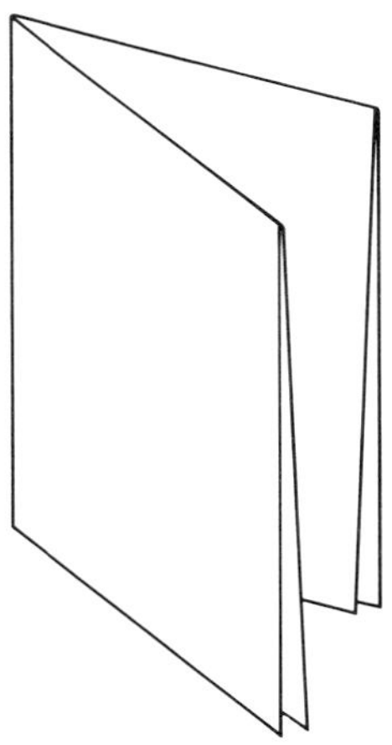

A3 folded in two directions
(French fold)
Four pages (A5) 148 x 210mm
Extravagant of paper but gives strength to a light or soft paper that has to stand up, eg invitations, menus, greetings cards. The sheet is printed on one side only but has the effect of a single fold printed on four sides.

Paper

Paper is important not only for its surface, which takes the printed image, but also for its weight and feel which can enhance or reduce the quality of the finished product.

Characteristics of paper

The choice of papers is very wide. For the desktop publisher the complexities of paper manufacture are less important than knowing the difference between the types of paper and when to use them.

In order to make a sensible choice of paper it is necessary to understand its main characteristics and what they mean to the printer and the reader.

Finish
Paper surfaces range from the very rough to the highly polished and glossy. The smoother the paper the better it is likely to accept fine details in offset printing, particularly of half-tone photographs. However, highly polished surfaces reflect the light badly which dazzles and irritates the reader. If half-tones are to be included a smooth but matt surface is likely to give the most satisfactory result.

Papers are sometimes described as having a 'top' and a 'wire' side. This refers to the faint pattern left by the wire mesh through which the pulp is drained. This does not normally present a problem for printing documents that are text only. In any case very many papers, particularly for offset printing, are so called 'twinwire', which means that they are equally good on both sides.

Opacity
Papers have different degrees of opacity or 'show-through'. Very thin, uncoated papers can be almost translucent while heavier stock can be completely opaque so that little or nothing can be seen of the printing on the other side of the sheet. Too much show-through can spoil a well laid out document, particularly if the pages include heavy rules, tint panels and half-tones. The opacity of paper can be assessed by laying a blank sheet over a printed page. If the type can be seen only very faintly then the show-through is probably acceptable. It will not always be possible to use a paper as opaque as you would like. It will frequently be a compromise between opacity, weight and cost.

Feel
Paper is a very tactile commodity. The way it feels in the hand can be important to the impression created by the finished document. It is always worth having a bound dummy made up in the paper you intend to use. From this you will be able to tell whether the publication is going to be too stiff or too floppy and how well it is going to open.It will not always be possible, or appropriate, to use a high quality paper that feels pleasant to the touch but for the occasional prestige job it is worth finding something better than the usual run-of-the-mill product.

Grain
The fibres of which a paper is made tend to lie parallel to the direction in which the pulp moves through the paper-making machine. This gives the paper its grain direction. Paper folds more readily in the direction of the grain so, wherever possible, the grain of the paper should run from top to bottom of the page. This gives a clean fold in the back of the document and ensures that the pages open well.

Finding the grain
It is usually the printer's responsibility to make sure that the grain of the paper runs the right way on the page but it is useful to be able to tell for yourself.

If the paper is watermarked, the grain runs from top to bottom of the sheet when the watermark is the right way up.

If, as is more likely, there is no water-mark, cut two strips from the sheet of paper, one from each direction, about 8 inches long and three-quarters of an inch wide. Hold them side by side and pointing upwards, between the finger and thumb. One strip will bend naturally much more than the other. The strip that stays more upright has the grain running along it; the one that bends has the grain running across it.

Weight

Paper weights are given in 'grams per square metre' (gsm). This does not mean much to anyone who is not handling paper every day.

Get some paper-maker's samples and use them as a reference to what a particular weight feels like.

As a *very* rough guide, the documents you might expect to find in the average office will probably be in the weight range:

writing papers 80-100 gsm
copying paper 70-90 gsm
32-page booklet 115-140 gsm
booklet cover 200-300 gsm
broadsheet newsletter 90-100 gsm

Cost

Paper can be an expensive material and there will be times when it will be worth getting comparative prices for similar stock. The important thing to remember is that the shorter the run the less important the paper cost is going to be. The difference in cost between printing five hundred copies on two different qualities of paper will be negligible, so use the better one. The final product will look and feel that much better for it.

Varieties of paper

Printers classify varieties of paper by name. It is useful to know broadly what they mean.

Uncoated cartridge

A strong, matt paper; not always pure white. Pleasant as a surface to read from. Good for continuous text and simple line drawings. Usually too rough a surface for half-tones unless it has been smoothed in manufacture (machine finished), in which case it will probably have lost some of its opacity and bulk.

Coated cartridge

A cartridge paper which has been coated with china clay to give greater smoothness. Usually whiter than uncoated papers. Gives excellent half-tone reproduction. Highly polished versions will reflect badly but matt surfaces avoid this and still give good half-tone reproduction.

Matt coated cartridge used in a laser printer gives a good quality original for offset plate-making.

Art paper

Sometimes called super calendered (SC). A very glossy paper with a highly polished coating of china clay. Originally intended for the reproduction of half-tones from metal blocks. Reflects the light badly and often feels unpleasantly slimy.

Antique

Uncoated with a matt, or even a rough, surface. Can be very pleasant to read from, with a comfortable feel. Some versions are made to be very bulky. If the surface is very soft or fluffy the printer may have difficulty using it on an offset press. (For the difference between wove and laid antiques see *Writing papers* below).

Writing papers

Writing papers are described as 'wove' or 'laid' depending on the type of wire covered roller (dandy roll) used to squeeze out the water from the thickening pulp during production.

Wove papers usually have an even surface with no obvious pattern visible in the paper itself if it is held up to the light, except for a water-mark if there is one.

Laid papers sometimes feel slightly ribbed and have a clear pattern of horizontal lines, crossed by more widely spaced vertical lines, visible against the light. The horizontal 'laid' lines usually run across the grain.

Most writing papers have a clearly distinguishable 'top' and 'wire' side.

Newsprint

As the name implies it is meant for newspapers. It is therefore cheap and lightweight, but tears easily and fades quickly. Not suitable for anything that has to survive for very long but ideal for short-lived publications such as in-house broadsheets. Its off-white colour and unashamed 'cheapness' have a particular attraction of their own when combined with strong, vigorous typography.

Copying paper

The surface of copying paper is specially finished to receive the toner used in copying machines and laser printers. It is not particularly pleasant to handle so unless a publication is to be produced entirely on a copying machine it is better to use a more general printing paper.

Paper sizes

British paper sizes were traditionally referred to by names (crown, demy, foolscap etc) which paper-makers and their customers understood. The operational needs of filing and continuous stationery have meant that this system has been very largely replaced by the ISO A series in which all sizes are geometrically related.

Trimmed sizes without bleed.

	mm	inches
A0	841 x 1189	33.1 x 46.8
A1	594 x 841	23.4 x 33.1
A2	420 x 594	16.5 x 23.4
A3	297 x 420	11.7 x 16.5
A4	210 x 297	8.3 x 11.7
A5	148 x 210	5.8 x 8.3
A6	105 x 148	4.1 x 5.8
A7	74 x 105	2.9 x 4.1
A8	52 x 74	2.1 x 2.9

Two other useful sizes are:

Two-thirds A4
210 x 198 8.3 x 7.8

One-third A4
210 x 99 8.3 x 3.9

Paper bought untrimmed from a paper merchant will be in SRA sizes which are larger to allow for bleed.

SRA0	900 x 1280	35.4 x 50.4
SRA1	640 x 900	25.2 x 35.4
SRA2	450 x 640	17.7 x 25.2
SRA3	320 x 450	12.6 x 17.7

Envelope sizes

Of the envelope sizes available to take documents in the international paper sizes the most useful are:
C4 which takes A4,
C5 which takes A5, and
DL which takes anything folded to one-third A4.

Below ISO A series (quarter size)

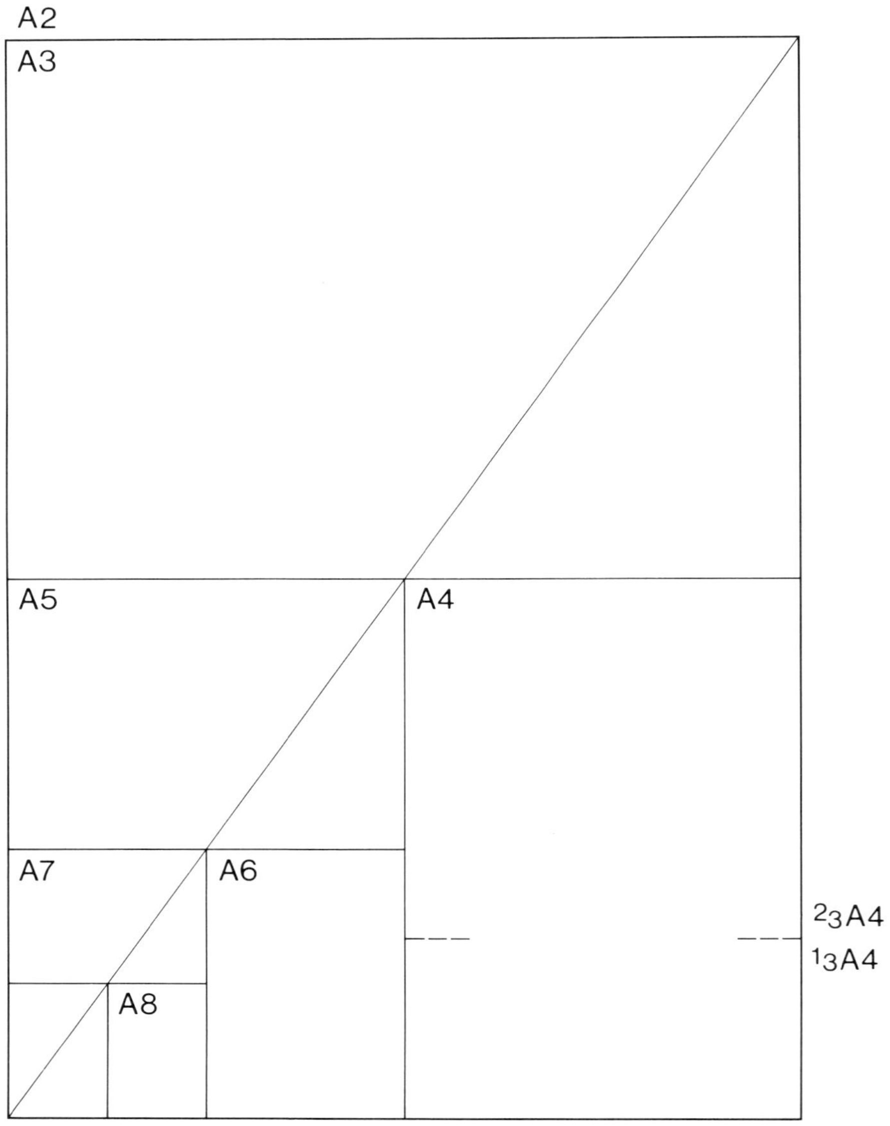

Reproduction in quantity

Designing and laying out the pages of a document are only steps on the way to reproducing it in quantity. The method of reproduction employed will largely depend on the number of copies needed.

Every time the original is copied there is a risk of some loss in quality.

Laser printer output

The printout from the laser printer is the best print you are going to get, unless the data is transferred to a high-resolution typesetting machine. If you want more than a few copies the laser printer is probably going to be too slow. In any case it can reproduce only one sheet printed on one side at a time. The more complicated the page make-up the longer it will take to emerge from the laser printer as the machine has to take time searching for different weights and sizes of type.

The surface of the paper used in laser printers and copiers is specially made to accept the toner used in the machines. A much sharper result can be obtained by using a thin (120gsm) blade-coated paper. The printed result will be better but the image will not bind well into the paper surface so the original must be handled with care.

Copying machines

Using a copying machine to reproduce the original can be a very economical method. Again this is particularly suitable for single sheet work, though many machines today will print on both sides of the sheet.

If the machine will take an A3 sheet and back up well on the other side, it is possible to make four-page A4 sections but the pairs of pages will have to be laid down carefully to ensure accurate margins.

When types are reproduced at a low resolution even the best copiers seem to lose some quality in reproduction, so for good quality and a long run it is best to use the laser printer output as an original for offset reproduction.

Offset printing

If the document is to be reproduced in a large quantity or is long enough to be bound in a number of sections, then it will almost certainly be reproduced by offset lithography, this usually means employing an outside printer.

In order to make the necessary printing plates, the original from the laser printer will have to be photographed. The printer will need clean, black and white originals. Once the originals have been put on film any corrections will be very expensive. The costs are even higher once plates have been made.

Make the most of the printer's professional skills. Call him in early and ask his advice as to the way he would like the material presented to make the best use of his presses. He will probably prefer to paste down and impose the original sheets himself and I should encourage him to do so.

Some of the decisions already made at the keyboard will make his task more or less difficult.

Remember that odd numbered pages (1,3,5...) always appear on a right-hand (recto) page, and even numbers on a left-hand (verso) page. The back margins on a verso page are on the right. On a recto page they come on the left.

Preparing artwork

Although many systems allow margins to be preset they are not always precisely accurate, so if a printout is being laid down for reproduction it is important to check the margins for each page and the alignment of columns. Sometimes the machine simply refuses to align columns on paper which look perfect on the screen. If the problem persists I prefer to cut the original and paste it in the correct position on the artwork rather than spend time getting cross with an inanimate machine.

To make manual corrections you will need a very sharp knife, rubber adhesive and thin white card. If there are more than a few pages to be pasted down, or if the page grid of the document is to be used again, then it is well worth having sheets of card pre-printed with the margins and column grid in pale blue. The original can then be pasted down accurately and photographed for reproduction. The blue guide lines will not be picked up by the camera.

How much skill?
Preparing artwork is a skilled job which calls for very precise and clean working methods. Some people are more adept than others.If it is not something that comes naturally to you, get a professional studio to help.

Planning ahead

Although your personal computer may be a very ingenious and sophisticated tool you will get the best results from it if you know what you want to achieve before you start.

A rough sketch layout can save a lot of time. Keep the first layout and compare it with the next one until you are fairly sure that you have got it right. Trial and error at the keyboard is expensive in time and frustration while you are waiting for the machine to catch up with your thoughts. The process can be made easier by making a few tools of the trade.

Is what you see what you want?

All designers and printers rely on manufacturer's type specimens and established measuring systems to plan layouts for print. Anyone preparing a document for desktop publishing needs the same sort of information.

Type specimens
The type fonts available on personal computers have different names. Some will have the same names as the fonts used by commercial printers such as 'Times' or 'Helvetica'. Because they have been produced at a low resolution each manufacturer will have assembled the bit map slightly differently so the result is inevitably a close approximation of the original (see *Digitised type*). Because the name doesn't really tell you very much it is important to know exactly what each typeface looks like and how much space each will occupy.

1 Keyboard a complete alphabet of each font - capitals, lower case, figures and punctuation.

2 Run it off in every size and weight available on your machine. Identify the name, size and weight each time. The laser printer will have to hunt for all the type variations, so printing out can take five minutes or more.

3 Keep each font on a separate sheet of paper and file them so that you can refer to them when you are planning layouts.

The same goes for rules and tint panels. Print out examples of everything that is available on your program and label them. In this way it will be possible to choose exactly what weight of rule to use and to compare it with the other weights available.

Type sizes Although manufacturers usually express type sizes in 'points' they are not always exactly the same. One manufacturer's 12 point might be slightly bigger or smaller than another's. It is therefore a good idea, particularly if the machine is new to you, to run off a few lines in various text sizes to see how much space they take up and file them with the other type specimens.

If only rather simple line spacing increments are available - single, double, triple - then set up specimens of those too.

Just as typeface measurements need checking, so column widths are not always what they seem. Scales of measurement which appear at the top of the screen may be in metric, imperial or points. Some programs give you a choice. In any case it is wise to run off a few lines in the width you have selected to make sure that it is accurate. It is not unusual to find that in order to get a 5-inch line the machine has to be set for 5 1/8".

For instance on the machine I am using, although the 10 point looks smaller than the 12 point, both their baselines are aligned on a 12 point body and so take up the same depth.

For instance on the machine I am using, the 10 point and 12 point are both aligned on a 12 point body and so take up the same depth

HELVETICA

9pt roman

ABCDEFGHIJKLMNOPQRSTUVWXYZ abcdefghijklmnopqrstuvwxyz
1234567890 - @£$%^&*§#()[]{} =+<>?:;,.~`'"

9pt bold

**ABCDEFGHIJKLMNOPQRSTUVWXYZabcdefghijklmnopqrstuvwxyz
1234567890 @£$%^&*§#()[]{} -=+<>?:;,.~`'"**

9pt italic

*ABCDEFGHIJKLMNOPQRSTUVWXYZabcdefghijklmnopqrstuvwxyz
1234567390 - @£$%^&*§#()[]{} =+<>?:;,.~`'"*

10pt roman

ABCDEFGHIJKLMNOPQRSTUVWXYZabcdefghijklmnopqrstuvwxyz
1234567890 @£$%^&*§#()[]{} -=+<>?:;,.~`'"

10pt bold

**ABCDEFGHIJKLMNOPQRSTUVWXYZabcdefghijklmnopqrstuvwxyz
1234567890 @£$%^&*§#()[]{} -=+<>?:;,.~`'"**

10pt italic

*ABCDEFGHIJKLMNOPQRSTUVWXYZabcdefghijklmnopqrstuvwxyz
1234567890 @£$%^&*§#()[]{} -=+<>?:;,.~`'"*

12pt roman

ABCDEFGHIJKLMNOPQRSTUVWXYZabcdefghijklmnopqrstuvwxyz
1234567890 @£$%^&*§#()[]{} -=+<>?:;,.~`'"

12pt bold

**ABCDEFGHIJKLMNOPQRSTUVWXYZabcdefghijklmnopqrstuvwxyz
1234567890 @£$%^&*§#()[]{} -=+<>?:;,.~`'"**

12pt italic

*ABCDEFGHIJKLMNOPQRSTUVWXYZabcdefghijklmnopqrstuvwxyz
1234567890 @£$%^&*§#()[]{} -=+<>?:;,.~`'"*

14pt roman

ABCDEFGHIJKLMNOPQRSTUVWXYZabcdefghijklmnopqrstuvwxyz
1234567890 @£$%^&*§#()[]{} -=+<>?:;,.~`'"

14pt bold

**ABCDEFGHIJKLMNOPQRSTUVWXYabcdefghijklmnopqrstuv
wxyz 1234567890 @£$%^&*§#()[]{} -=+<>?:;,.~`'"**

14pt italic

*ABCDEFGHIJKLMNOPQRSTUVWXYZ
abcdefghijklmnopqrstuvwxyz1234567890 @£$%^&*()[]{}-=+<>?:;,.'"*

TIMES

9pt roman

ABCDEFGHIJKLMNOPQRSTUVWXYZ abcdefghijklmnopqrstuvwxyz
1234567890 - @£$%^&*§#()[]{} =+<>?:;,.~`'"

9pt bold

ABCDEFGHIJKLMNOPQRSTUVWXYZabcdefghijklmnopqrstuvwxyz
1234567890 @£$%^&*§#()[]{} -=+<>?:;,.~`'"

9pt italic

ABCDEFGHIJKLMNOPQRSTUVWXYZabcdefghijklmnopqrstuvwxyz
1234567890 - @£$%^&§#()[]{} =+<>?:;,.~`'"*

10pt roman

ABCDEFGHIJKLMNOPQRSTUVWXYZabcdefghijklmnopqrstuvwxyz
1234567890 @£$%^&*§#()[]{} -=+<>?:;,.~`'"

10pt bold

ABCDEFGHIJKLMNOPQRSTUVWXYZabcdefghijklmnopqrstuvwxyz
1234567890 @£$%^&*§#()[]{} -=+<>?:;,.~`'"

10pt italic

ABCDEFGHIJKLMNOPQRSTUVWXYZabcdefghijklmnopqrstuvwxyz
1234567890 @£$%^&§#()[]{} -=+<>?:;,.~`'"*

12pt roman

ABCDEFGHIJKLMNOPQRSTUVWXYZabcdefghijklmnopqrstuvwxyz
1234567890 @£$%^&*§#()[]{} -=+<>?:;,.~`'"

12pt bold

ABCDEFGHIJKLMNOPQRSTUVWXYZabcdefghijklmnopqrstuvwxyz
1234567890 @£$%^&*§#()[]{} -=+<>?:;,.~`'"

12pt italic

ABCDEFGHIJKLMNOPQRSTUVWXYZabcdefghijklmnopqrstuvwxyz
1234567890 @£$%^&§#()[]{} -=+<>?:;,.~`'"*

14pt roman

ABCDEFGHIJKLMNOPQRSTUVWXYZabcdefghijklmnopqrstuvwxyz
1234567890 @£$%^&*§#()[]{} -=+<>?:;,.~`'"

14pt bold

ABCDEFGHIJKLMNOPQRSTUVWXYZ
abcdefghijklmnopqrstuvwxyz
1234567890 @£$%^&*§#()[]{} -=+<>?:;,.~`'"

14pt italic

ABCDEFGHIJKLMNOPQRSTUVWXYZ
abcdefghijklmnopqrstuvwxyz
1234567890 - @£$%^&§#()[]{} =+<>?:;,.~`'"*

18pt roman

ABCDEFGHIJKLMNOPQRSTUVWXYZ
abcdefghijklmnopqrstuvwxyz
1234567890 @£$%^&*§#()[]{} -=+<>?:;,.~`'"

18pt bold

ABCDEFGHIJKLMNOPQRSTUVWXYZ
abcdefghijklmnopqrstuvwxyz
1234567890 @£$%^&*§#()[]{} -=+<>?:;,.~`'"

18pt italic

ABCDEFGHIJKLMNOPQRSTUVWXYZ
abcdefghijklmnopqrstuvwxyz
1234567890 @£$%^&§#()[]{} -=+<>?:;,.~`'"*

24pt roman

ABCDEFGHIJKLMNOPQRSTUVWXYZ
abcdefghijklmnopqrstuvwxyz
1234567890 @£$%^&*§#()[]{} -=+<>?:;,.~

24pt bold

ABCDEFGHIJKLMNOPQRSTUVWX
abcdefghijklmnopqrstuvwxyz
1234567890 @£$%^&*§#()[]{}-=+

24pt italic

ABCDEFGHIJKLMNOPQRSTUVWXYZ
abcdefghijklmnopqrstuvwxyz
1234567890 @£$%^&§#()[]{} -=+<>?:;,.*

24pt shadow

ABCDEFGHIJKLMNOPQRSTUVWX
abcdefghijklmnopqrstuvwxyz
1234567890 @£$%^&*§#()[]{} -=+<

24pt shadow bold

ABCDEFGHIJKLMNOPQRSTUV
abcdefghijklmnopqrstuvwxyz
1234567890 @£$%&*§#()[]{}=+

24pt outline

ABCDEFGHIJKLMNOPQRSTUVWX
abcdefghijklmnopqrstuvwxyz
1234567890 @£$%^&*§#()[]{}-=+

24pt outline bold

ABCDEFGHIJKLMNOPQRSTUV
abcdefghijklmnopqrstuvwxyz
1234567890 @£$%&*§#()[]{}=+

Pencil layouts

Although the program may allow you to see the whole page or even a spread on the screen, it is still often quicker and more satisfactory to make pencil layouts first so that you have some idea of how the document is going to fit together. These do not have to be very elaborate or highly finished. They are merely preliminary working drawings which allow you to make some basic decisions before you commit yourself to page makeup. It will not be necessary to make such layouts for the whole document. Once the page depth, column widths, headings and subheadings have been established then the rest can be done on the screen.

Make your own line counter
A line counter is a great help in sketching page layouts.

1 Select the type size and line spacing you intend to use for most of the text.

2 Using an underlining rule, set up enough blank lines at that size to fill a full column, numbering each line.

3 Set an x at the beginning and end of each line to record the x-height.

With this line counter under a piece of tracing paper, rough but accurate layouts can be tried out very quickly. It is also possible to get a very good idea of just how long the document is going to be.

01x__________x
02x__________x
03x__________x
04x__________x
05x__________x
06x__________x
07x__________x
08x__________x
09x__________x
10x__________x
11x__________x
12x__________x
13x__________x
14x__________x
15x__________x
16x__________x
17x__________x
18x__________x
19x__________x
20x__________x
21x__________x
22x__________x
23x__________x
24x__________x
25x__________x
26x__________x
27x__________x
28x__________x
29x__________x
30x__________x
31x__________x
32x__________x
33x__________x
34x__________x
35x__________x
36x__________x
37x__________x
38x__________x
39x__________x
40x__________x
41x__________x
42x__________x
43x__________x
44x__________x
45x__________x
46x__________x
47x__________x
48x__________x
49x__________x
50x__________x
51x__________x
52x__________x
53x__________x
54x__________x
55x__________x
56x__________x
57x__________x
58x__________x
59x__________x
60x__________x
61x__________x
62x__________x
63x__________x

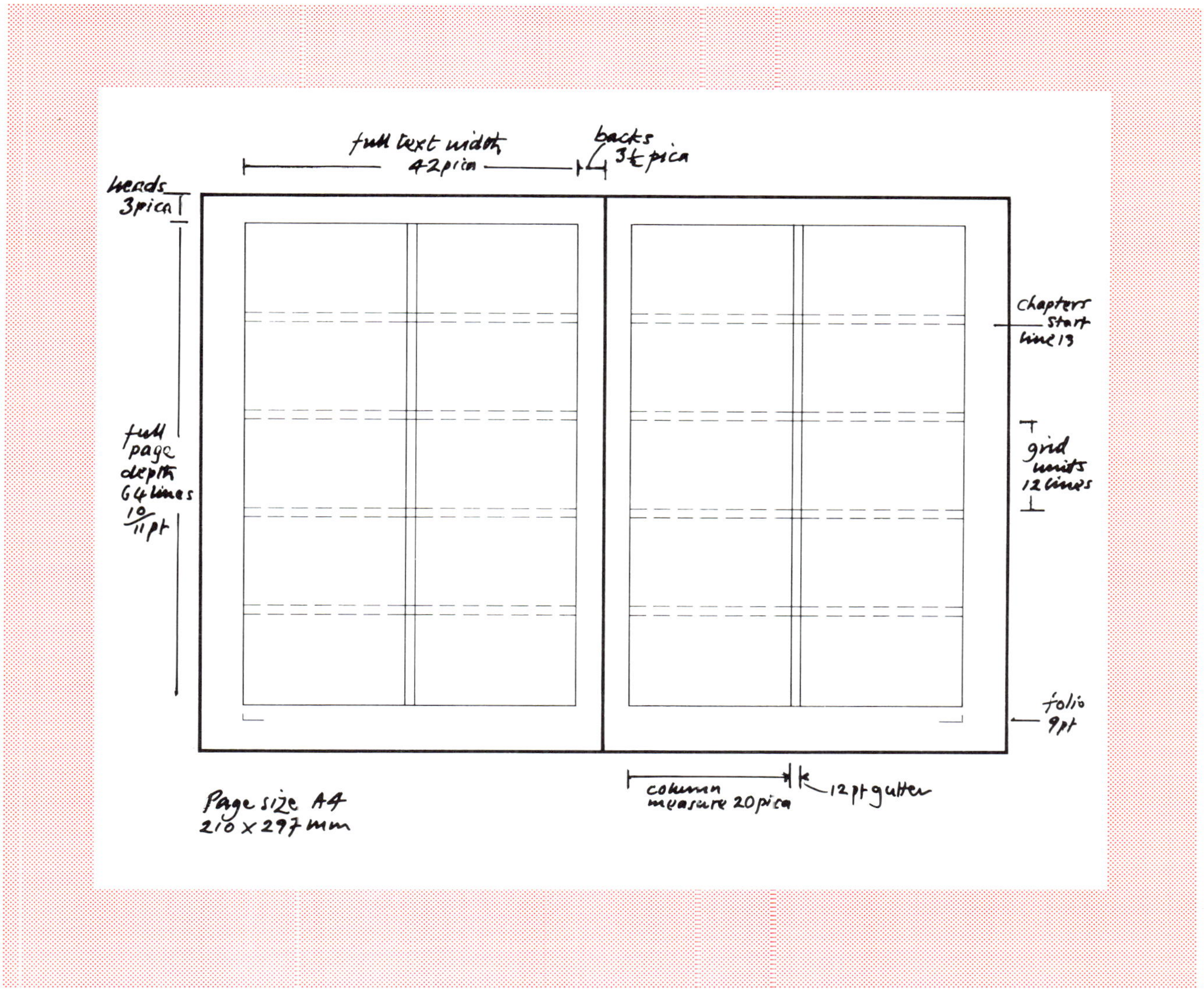

Grid sheets

Whether or not page make-up on the screen is available to you, a grid sheet is an invaluable tool. It is helpful to have two; one drawn on card or cartridge paper, to go under transparent paper when making pencil sketches; and a second grid on film to lay over the page printout to check alignment.

The grid sheets must be drawn accurately. As you are likely to use the same grid again for another publication, keep the original and make PMT copies. Ordinary photo-copies may not be accurate enough because the paper shrinks or expands as it gets warm under the lights.

A typical annotated grid sheet for a two-column layout.

Keep the margin specifications separate from the text measures and leave the grid itself clear.

Examples of pencil sketches

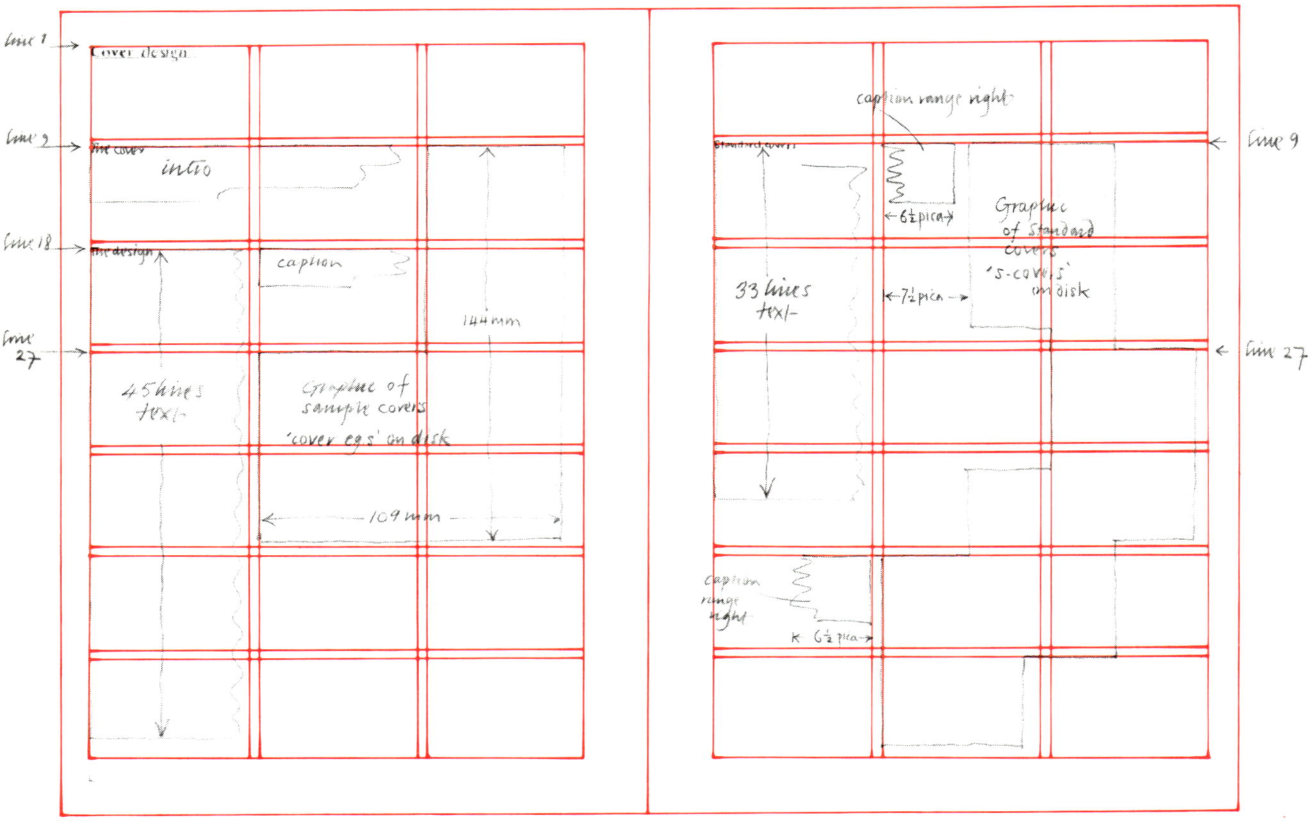

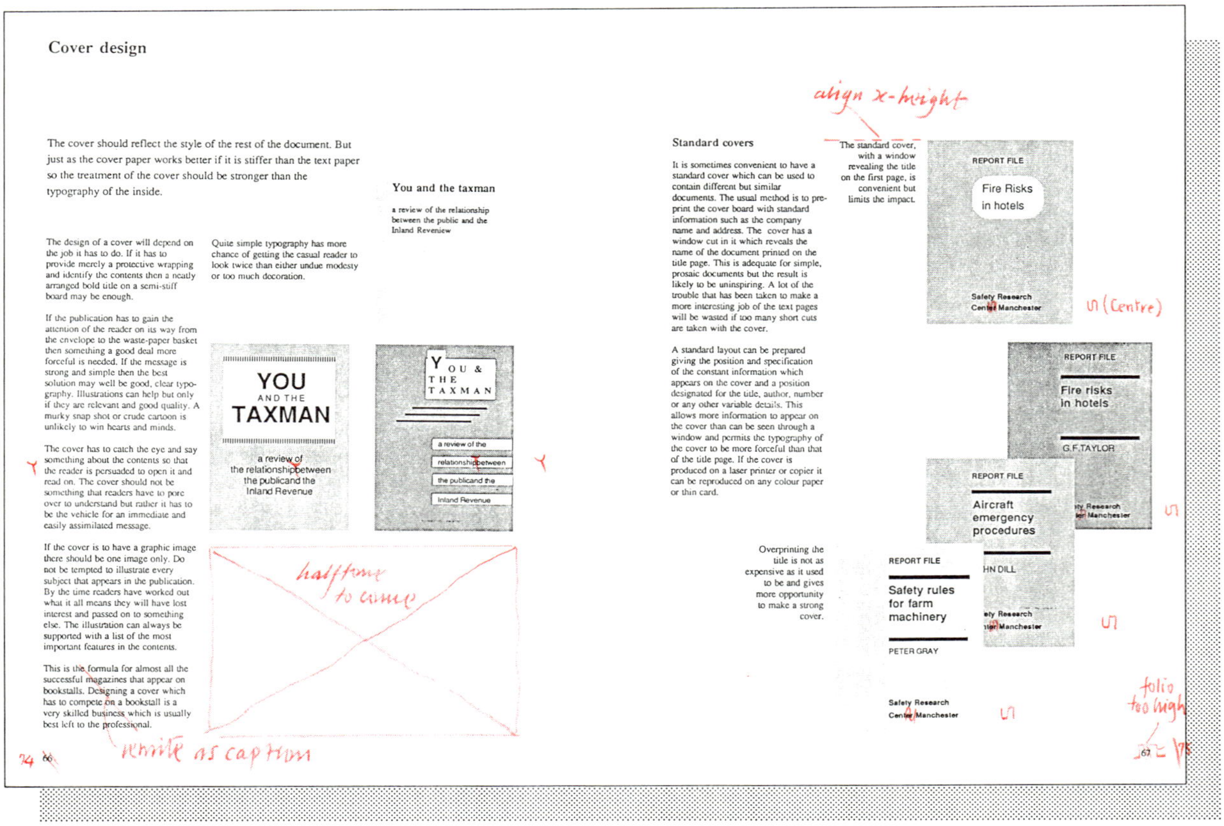

Cover design

The cover should reflect the style of the rest of the document. But just as the cover paper works better if it is stiffer than the text paper so the treatment of the cover should be stronger than the typography of the inside.

The design of a cover will depend on the job it has to do. If it has to provide merely a protective wrapping and identify the contents then a neatly arranged bold title on a semi-stiff board may be enough.

If the publication has to gain the attention of the reader on its way from the envelope to the waste-paper basket then something a good deal more forceful is needed. If the message is strong and simple then the best solution may well be good, clear typography. Illustrations can help but only if they are relevant and good quality. A murky snap shot or crude cartoon is unlikely to win hearts and minds.

The cover has to catch the eye and say something about the contents so that the reader is persuaded to open it and read on. The cover should not be something that readers have to pore over to understand but rather it has to be the vehicle for an immediate and easily assimilated message.

If the cover is to have a graphic image there should be one image only. Do not be tempted to illustrate every subject that appears in the publication. By the time readers have worked out what it all means they will have lost interest and passed on to something else. The illustration can always be supported with a list of the most important features in the contents.

This is the formula for almost all the successful magazines that appear on bookstalls. Designing a cover which has to compete on a bookstall is a very skilled business which is usually best left to the professional.

Quite simple typography has more chance of getting the casual reader to look twice than either undue modesty or too much decoration.

You and the taxman

a review of the relationship between the public and the Inland Revenue

Standard covers

It is sometimes convenient to have a standard cover which can be used to contain different but similar documents. The usual method is to pre-print the cover board with standard information such as the company name and address. The cover has a window cut in it which reveals the name of the document printed on the title page. This is adequate for simple, prosaic documents but the result is likely to be uninspiring. A lot of the trouble that has been taken to make a more interesting job of the text pages will be wasted if too many short cuts are taken with the cover.

A standard layout can be prepared giving the position and specification of the constant information which appears on the cover and a position designated for the title, author, number or any other variable details. This allows more information to appear on the cover than can be seen through a window and permits the typography of the cover to be more forceful than that of the title page. If the cover is produced on a laser printer or copier it can be reproduced on any colour paper or thin card.

The standard cover, with a window revealing the title on the first page, is convenient but limits the impact.

Overprinting the title is not as expensive as it used to be and gives more opportunity to make a strong cover.

The first printout will probably not be exactly as you want it. Check the hard copy against the grid and make the corrections.

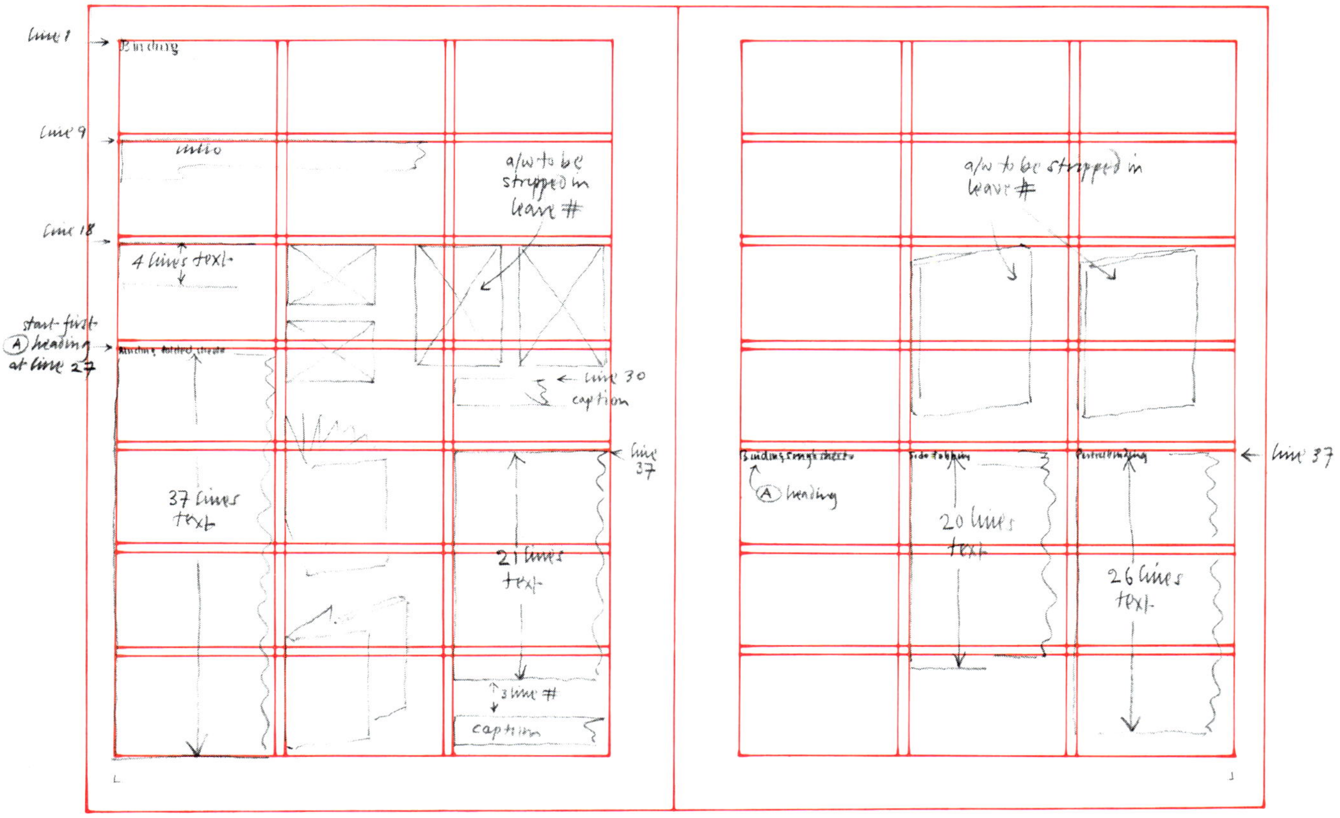

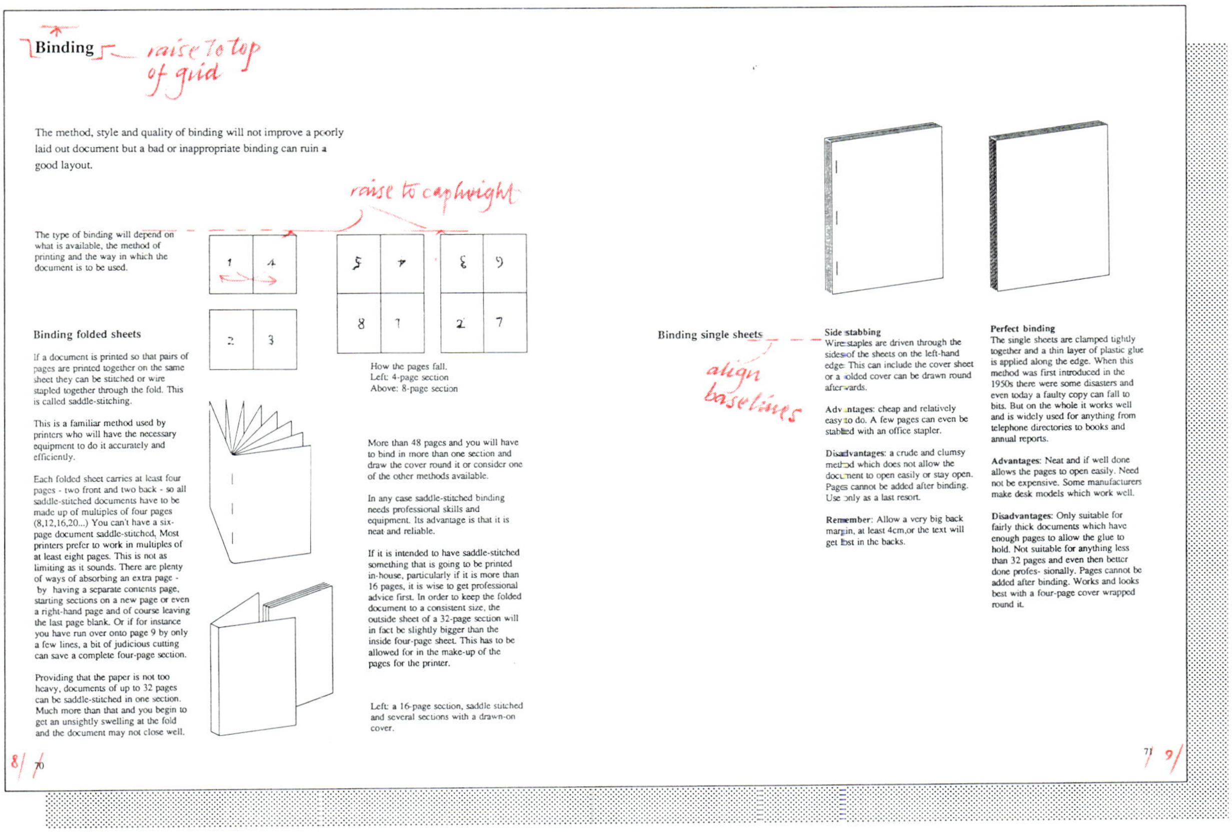

Binding

raise to top of grid

The method, style and quality of binding will not improve a poorly laid out document but a bad or inappropriate binding can ruin a good layout.

raise to capheight

The type of binding will depend on what is available, the method of printing and the way in which the document is to be used.

Binding folded sheets

If a document is printed so that pairs of pages are printed together on the same sheet they can be stitched or wire stapled together through the fold. This is called saddle-stitching.

This is a familiar method used by printers who will have the necessary equipment to do it accurately and efficiently.

Each folded sheet carries at least four pages - two front and two back - so all saddle-stitched documents have to be made up of multiples of four pages (8,12,16,20...) You can't have a six-page document saddle-stitched, Most printers prefer to work in multiples of at least eight pages. This is not as limiting as it sounds. There are plenty of ways of absorbing an extra page - by having a separate contents page, starting sections on a new page or even a right-hand page and of course leaving the last page blank. Or if for instance you have run over onto page 9 by only a few lines, a bit of judicious cutting can save a complete four-page section.

Providing that the paper is not too heavy, documents of up to 32 pages can be saddle-stitched in one section. Much more than that and you begin to get an unsightly swelling at the fold and the document may not close well.

How the pages fall.
Left: 4-page section
Above: 8-page section

More than 48 pages and you will have to bind in more than one section and draw the cover round it or consider one of the other methods available.

In any case saddle-stitched binding needs professional skills and equipment. Its advantage is that it is neat and reliable.

If it is intended to have saddle-stitched something that is going to be printed in-house, particularly if it is more than 16 pages, it is wise to get professional advice first. In order to keep the folded document to a consistent size, the outside sheet of a 32-page section will in fact be slightly bigger than the inside four-page sheet. This has to be allowed for in the make-up of the pages for the printer.

Left: a 16-page section, saddle stitched and several sections with a drawn-on cover.

8/ 70

Binding single sheets

align baselines

Side stabbing
Wire staples are driven through the sides of the sheets on the left-hand edge. This can include the cover sheet or a folded cover can be drawn round afterwards.

Advantages: cheap and relatively easy to do. A few pages can even be stabbed with an office stapler.

Disadvantages: a crude and clumsy method which does not allow the document to open easily or stay open. Pages cannot be added after binding. Use only as a last resort.

Remember: Allow a very big back margin, at least 4cm,or the text will get lost in the backs.

Perfect binding
The single sheets are clamped tightly together and a thin layer of plastic glue is applied along the edge. When this method was first introduced in the 1950s there were some disasters and even today a faulty copy can fall to bits. But on the whole it works well and is widely used for anything from telephone directories to books and annual reports.

Advantages: Neat and if well done allows the pages to open easily. Need not be expensive. Some manufacturers make desk models which work well.

Disadvantages: Only suitable for fairly thick documents which have enough pages to allow the glue to hold. Not suitable for anything less than 32 pages and even then better done profes- sionally. Pages cannot be added after binding. Works and looks best with a four-page cover wrapped round it.

71 9/

Establishing standards

Type specimens and line counters make it easier to plan the work. A record of the solution ensures that the time and effort expended are not dissipated.

Keep a written and illustrated specification for each publication noting the typeface and size, measure (column width), margins, grid and subheading system. A standard form will ensure that nothing is forgotten and will be invaluable if:

- The job has to be picked up again after a break or by another operator.
- A new, revised edition is wanted.
- The formula has to be repeated for a similar document.

Although such information will be stored on disc, it helps to keep a set as hard copy in a ring binder. This will allow you to see exactly what you are going to get on paper. It is also useful to record examples of headings, quotes and any graphic elements that might be worth repeating; and where they are stored.

It is good practice to establish a consistent style for like publications coming from the same organisation. To this end a simple style manual can record precedents for ways in which things are to be done. This makes for consistency and saves reinventing the wheel every time a new document is started.

But not all documents are alike and they will not all be used in the same way. Any solution can be improved upon and there will be a need for change from time to time. Style manuals should be reviewed occasionally and not treated as so sacred a text that good ideas for improvement are considered heretical.

Style manuals do not have to be very elaborate. Quite a small amount of information will help to maintain a constant standard.

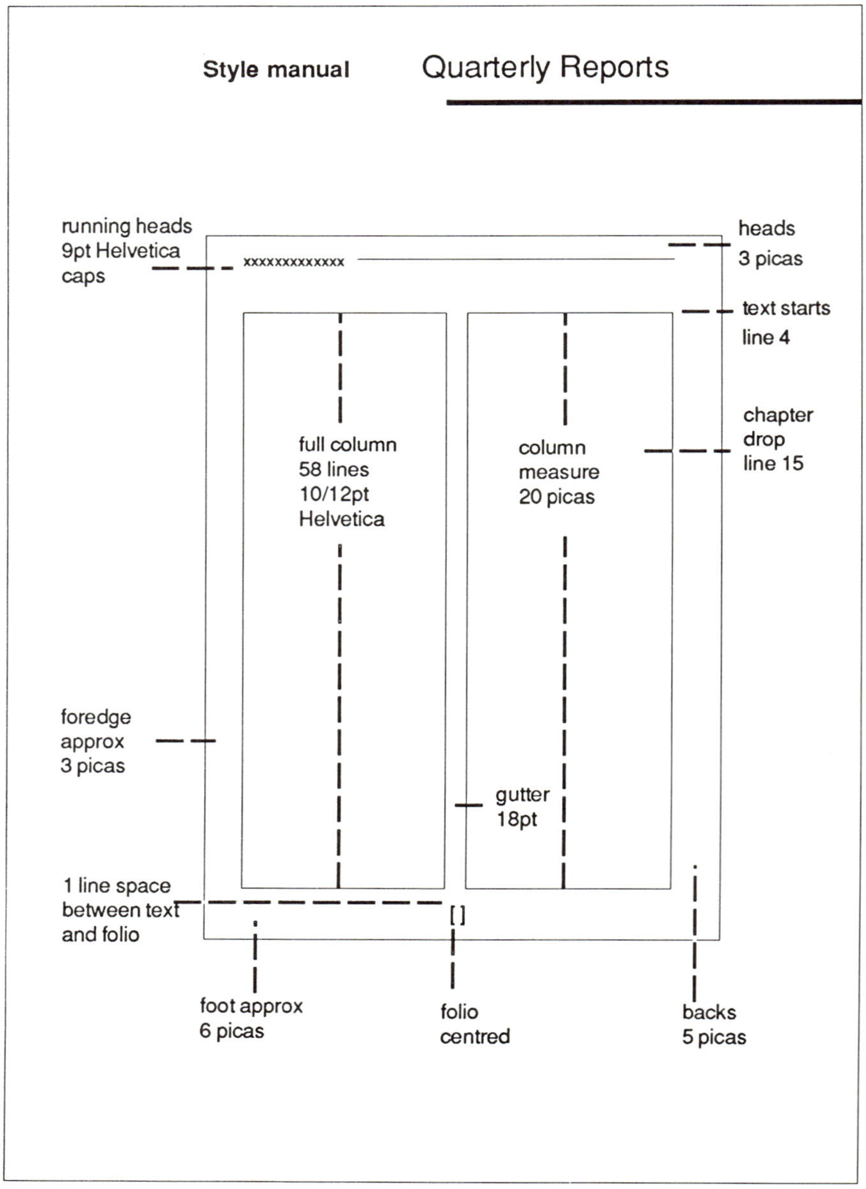

Sample specification

		samples
Title	Design for Desktop Publishing	
Author	John Miles	
Format	A4 210 x 297 mm	
Typeface	Times (Mac version)	
Text size	10 point on 12 point body range left	This is a sample of 10 point Times set on a 12 point body. To be used as the text for this publication
Full page depth	62 lines of 10 on 12 point	
Full page width	41 picas	
Column widths	2 col 20 pica with 1 pica between cols 3 col 13 pica with 1 pica between cols	
Horizontal grid	7 units of 8 lines each with 1 line between	
Margins	head 3 pica 6 points foot (excluding folio) 5 pica 6 points backs 5 pica foredge 3 pica 4 points (approx)	
Chapter titles	18 point Times bold u&lc	**Chapter**
Intro paragraph	12 point Times 27 pica wide start line no 9	Type size for introduction copy
Chapters start	line no 17	
Subheads	**A** - 12 point bold occupying 4 lines of text	last line of paragraph *2 line space* **Subhead A** *1 line space* First line of next para
	B - 10 point bold occupying 2 lines of text	last line of paragraph *1 line space* **Subhead B** First line of next para
	C - 10 point bold run on after one line space	last line of para *1 line space* **Subhead C** starts line
Folios	in foot margin, full out left and right 1 line space between text and figures	
Captions	10 point Times to 13 pica or 6 pica as necessary	
Prelim pages	see annotated proofs in file	

Some of the printer's marks used in the UK

Correcting copy

Every typist or keyboard operator makes mistakes and so can the computer. These are usually minor *literals* in spelling, punctuation or word order. It is extremely difficult for the operator to see all these himself, he is just too close to the job. It is therefore essential that somebody else reads the keyboarded copy, preferably before it is made up into pages and certainly before anything is pasted down for printing. This is an aspect of copy preparation for which there are as yet no short cuts. Someone has systematically to compare the keyboarded text with some sort of original whether it be manuscript, typescript or from a dictaphone. If the original text is coded for typographical instructions then it may be necessary to compare the original text with hard copy printout.

Too many unnoticed literals in a text can reduce its authority as much as good presentation can add to it.

The printing industry has an established standard of correction marks. It would be wise to adopt the same standards for desktop publishing.

Printing and personal computers are already becoming part of the same communications industry and the more language they have in common the better.

instruction	mark in text	mark in margin
leave unchanged	desktop publishing	✓ or stet
insert new copy	publishing	desktop
delete (remove)	desktop publishing	
close up	desk top publishing	
delete and close up	deskstop publishing	
insert space	desktoppublishing	or #
reduce space	desktop publishing	
substitute characters	desktip publishing	o/
wrong font (typeface)	desktop publishing	×
set in italic	desktop publishing	
set in capitals	desktop publishing	
set in small caps	desktop publishing	
set in bold	desktop publishing	
set in bold italic	desktop publishing	
set in lower case	DESKtop publishing	
set in roman	*desktop* publishing	
invert	doʇʞsǝp publishing	
spell out in full	2 desktops	spell out
inser full point (stop)	desktop publishing	
insert colon	desktop publishing	
insert semi-colon	desktop publishing	;
insert coma	desktop publishing	,
insert quote marks	desktop publishing	
insert double quotes	desktop publishing	
insert apostrophe	desktop publishers	
insert hyphen	desktop publishing	
start new paragraph	desktop publishing. The best way...	or n.p.
run on	desktop publishing. The best way...	or run on

transpose words	publ shing desktop	or Trs
transpose lines	publ shing desktop	
centre type	desktop publishing	[ ] or centre
move right (indent)	desktop publishing	
move left	desktop publishing	
take over to next line	desktop publishing	t.o.
take back to next line	desktop publishing	t.b
raise	desktop publishing	
lower	desktop publishing	

Everything can make mistakes

Glossary

These are just a few of the technical terms that newcomers to printing, through desktop publishing, are likely to encounter. The definitions have been kept deliberately brief.

A

Ampersand, the sign '&' meaning 'and'.

Antique paper, an uncoated paper with a matt or rough surface.

Arabic figures, the familiar form of numerals: 1 2 3 4 etc. Cf. *Roman figures*.

Art paper, glossy, coated paper intended to carry halftone reproduction by *letterpress*.

Artwork, any black and white or colour original prepared for reproduction. Also called *mechanicals* in USA.

Ascender, the vertical stroke, above the x-height, in lower case letters such as b d h.

Asterisk, the sign *.

Asymmetric layout, an off-centre arrangement.

B

Backing up, printing the second side of a sheet, ideally so that the lines on one side match the position of those on the other.

Backs, the margin on a page nearest to the fold.

Banner, in newspaper work, a main headline running across the top of the page. Often used more loosely for the title heading on a journal or newspaper.

Baseline, (type) the line on which both capitals (H) and lower case (x) letters stand.

Bleed, the area of illustrations, solids or rules which extend beyond the trimmed edge of a printed page *and* the extra width added to artwork to make bleeding possible.

Blobs, solid discs (●).

Body, (type) the space, measured from top to bottom, on which a letter is set.

Bold, the heavy version of a particular typeface.

Bolts, the edges of a folded section of paper before it is trimmed.

Book, (type) the medium weight of a typeface intended for continuous text. (More commonly used in USA).

Bowl, the curved part of rounded letters such as B R b p.

Box, text ruled off on all four sides.

Braces, { }.

Brackets, [ ] sometimes called 'square brackets'. See *parentheses*.

Broadsheet or *broadside*, technically something printed on a full-size sheet. Commonly used to refer to documents of large newspaper size.

Bulk, thickness of paper in single sheets or as the pages of a document.

C

Cannon balls, see *blobs*.

Cap height, the height of capital letters in a fount of type.

Caption, text describing an illustration.

Centre-spread, the pair of pages that come at the centre of a folded section (eg pages 4 and 5 in an 8-page section).

Character, an individual letter in a fount of type.

Coated paper, one with a surface finished with a layer of china clay to give smoothness.

Collating, gathering pages or sections in the correct order.

Colophon, text giving production details of a document. Sometimes used, incorrectly, for a publisher's trade mark.

Column rule, a fine rule used to separate columns of text.

Continuous tone, see *halftone*.

Copy, (computers) to store a duplicate; (print) the original manuscript or typescript from which text is to be keyboarded.

Correction marks, conventional signs used by printers, editors and designers to indicate typographic changes.

Counter, (type) the white area inside characters such as B D O d q.

Cover, the outside pages of a document.

Cropping, cutting an illustration to fit a given area or to remove unwanted background along the edges.

Cross reference, using typographic symbols to refer the reader to relevant text within the same document.

Crosshead, a centred subheading, see *subhead*.

Cut flush, trimming the cover of a document at the same time and to the same size as the inside pages.

Cut out, a photograph from which all the background has been removed.

D

Deckle-edge, the rough, uncut edge on hand- or mould-made papers.

Delete, to remove or erase.

Descender, the part of the letter which comes below the baseline, in lower case letters such as g p q y etc.

Digitising, converting the shape of a character into coded data in a computer.

Display, (type) large sizes or ornate forms not normally used for continuous text; (layout) the use of large type, rules and other devices to present information.

Drawn-on cover, a card cover fixed to the spine of a publication.

Drop, (chapter) the distance from a chapter title to first line of text.

Drop-shadow, a tint or solid laid to one side of an illustration or type form to give a shadow effect.

Dry-transfer, adhesive lettering or symbols which can be added to artwork by hand.

E

Earpiece, small advertisements that appear in the top corners of newspapers and broadsheet publications.

Em, the square of the body of a type. Sometimes called a 'mutton'.

En, half the square of the body of a type. Sometimes called a 'nut'.

End paper, leaves that join the text of a book to the binding, see *self-ends*.

Extended/expanded, a wide version of a particular typeface.

F

Family, (type) a series of alphabets in different weights with the same design characteristics.

Folio, page number.

Foot, the margin at the bottom of a page

Foredge, the outer, vertical edge of a page.

Format, (printing) the trimmed size of a document, eg A4 format. (PC) the arrangement of the text on a page.

Fount (UK) or *Font* (US), in printing the total characters in a complete typeface, caps, lower case, figures and punctuation. In PC jargon usually just means typeface.

Full out left, text set to the left-hand edge of the column, without indent.

Full point, printer's term for a full stop.

G

Galley proofs, text proofed in continuous columns, not divided into pages.

Gate fold, a single sheet of paper folded twice vertically to make six pages.

Gather, see *collating*.

Grain, the direction in which a sheet of paper is made and along which it folds most readily.

Grid, the rectangular structure of a page layout.

Gutter, the space between columns.

H

H and J, hyphenation and justification.

Half-title, the first page of a book, usually attached to the front endpaper, *or* pages dividing sections within a document.

Halftone, a photograph broken up into fine dots for reproduction.

Hanging indent, text with the first line set full out to the left and subsequent lines indented.

Head, the top margin on a page.

Hot metal, strictly type from a casting machine but widely used for any type set in relief on a metal body. See *letterpress*.

Hue, colour.

Hyphenation, breaking a word at the end of a line, followed by a hyphen (-), to give even word spacing.

I

Imposition, the arrangement of pages on a printing plate so that when the sheet is folded the sequence of pages is correct.

Imprint, printed bibliographical and copyright information. Also the term used for the issuing publisher.

Indent, space inserted at the beginning of a line(s).

Inferior figures, small numerals which appear below the baseline. Sometimes called 'subscript' on PCs, see *superior figures*.

Initial letter, a single letter, bigger than the text, usually used to mark the beginning of a chapter or section.

Italic, the sloped version of a typeface.

J

Justification, spacing out the words in a line so that all the lines in the column come to the same length, see *unjustified.*

K

Kern, part of a character that overhangs another to aid even spacing.

L

Laid, paper with a clearly visible wire pattern.

Landscape, a document that is wider than it is high.

Layout, the arrangement of text and images on a page.

Leaders, dotted lines .... intended to lead the reader's eye from one piece of text to another.

Leading, see *line feed.*

Leaf, a single sheet in a document with one page on each side, eg an eight-page booklet has four leaves.

Legibility, a quality of a typeface depending on how easy it is to read. See *readability.*

Letter spacing, wider than normal space between characters within a word.

Letterpress, printing from relief type.

Ligature, two or more characters joined together to ensure even spacing. Rarely found on PC output.

Line feed, space between lines of text, sometimes called *leading.*

Line illustration, those made up of lines and solid areas, without continuous tone.

Lining figures, numerals that align with the capitals. Non-lining or hanging figures, which are based on the lower case x-height, are not normally available on PCs.

Literal, a misprint.

Logotype or *logo,* a word or name rendered in a specific way as in a trademark. Not to be confused with a symbol.

Lower case, the small characters in a fount of type: a b c d etc.

M

Margins, the area of paper between the text and the edges of a page.

Measure, the width of a column of text.

Mechanicals, see *artwork.*

N

Newsprint, a cheap paper intended for newspapers and ephemeral journals.

Non-lining figures, see *lining figures.*

O

Offset lithography, usually shortened to 'offset'. A process of printing from a flat surface in which the printing areas are greasy and the non-printing areas are damp. The greasy and inked image is set off from the printing plate onto a rubber blanket which transfers it to the paper.

Opacity, the degree to which a paper is translucent.

Opening, see *spread.*

Outline letter, a letterform that is drawn in outline only with no solid parts.

Overmatter, copy too long to fit the text area and so will have to be cut.

P

Page, one side of a leaf. *To page*, dividing galley proofs (and illustrations) into pages.

Page depth, the length of the text area on the page.

Parentheses, ( ). See *brackets* and *braces.*

Paste-up, type proofs and illustrations stuck down together as a guide.

Perfect binding, a method of binding single leaves by gluing them together on one edge.

Pica, a unit of typographical measurement = 12 points.

Pixels, the individual elements into which images are broken down when they are digitised.

Point, the basic unit of typographic measurement.

Portrait, the shape of a document that is deeper than it is wide.

Prelims, the opening or 'preliminary pages' of a document before the text proper starts.

Proof, a trial print to be checked for corrections.

Q

Quarto, a page a quarter the size of the basic sheet.

Quotes, marks which indicate speech. They can be 'single' or "double".

R

Range left/right, align type to the left or right, leaving the other edge ragged.

Readability, a function of how type is used. Given a legible type, the readability of a page will depend as much upon the layout as on the typeface.

Recto, a right-hand page.

Register, the exact positioning of two or more printings on a sheet.

Register marks, crosses or sight marks on artwork or a printed sheet to ensure accurate register.

Resolution, sharpness of definition of a digitised image depending on the number of scan lines to the inch.

Retouching, manual adjustment to an illustration or other image.

Reversing out, printing a white image on a solid background or tint panel.

Revise, a corrected proof or the act of proof correction.

Ring binder, a ready-made, stiff folder with metal binding rings.

Rivers, white lines appearing to run vertically through a text paragraph.

Roman figures, I II III IV etc. See *arabic figures*.

Rules, lines of various thickness and pattern used to divide and box text on a page.

Run, the number of copies to be printed.

Run on (printing) extra copies printed at the same time as the original run; (typesetting) text continuing on the same line.

Running head, a small headline repeated at the top of each page.

S

Saddle-stitch, bind by passing a wire or thread through the centre of a folded section.

Sanserif, a typeface without serifs.

Scale, to measure and specify illustrations to fit a layout.

Score, to mark card with a blunt blade along the line of a fold before creasing to prevent cracking.

Section, a printed sheet folded to page size.

Self-cover, a cover of the same paper as the rest of the document.

Self-ends, the first and last pages of a document used to attach it to the binding, see *end papers*.

Semi-bold, a weight of a typeface a little heavier than the normal text version but not as heavy as a bold.

Serif, the small terminal stroke at the end of the main stroke of a letter.

Set, to assemble letters into words and lines, *or* the width of an individual character across the body.

Set solid, type set without any extra space between the lines.

Shadow letter, a letterform with extra weight down one side giving a shadow effect.

Show-through, the degree to which the print on one side of a sheet can be seen from the other side.

Side heading, a subheading in the side margin.

Side stab, bind by passing wire staples through the side of the bound edge

Small caps, capital letters specially drawn to range with the lower case x-height.

Solid, 100 per cent tint panel unbroken by dots or lines.

Solidus, oblique stroke /.

Spine, the bound edge.

Spread, a pair of facing pages.

Square up, to specify an illustration as a rectangle. Cf *cut out*.

Stress, (type) the apparent direction of the weight of a letter from the vertical to the oblique.

Subheading, a heading appearing within the body of the text.

Superior figures, small numerals appearing above the x-height. Sometimes called 'superscript' on PCs.

Swash, characters with additional flourishes.

T

Tabloid, a page half the size of a broadsheet. A format frequently used for house journals.

Tint, a flat area made up of dots or lines.

Tip in, an illustration pasted onto a page after printing. Usually glued along one edge.

Title page, first or third page in a document giving the title of the work, the author and publisher.

Tone, the strength of a colour from solid to light.

Trim, to cut the edges of a folded sheet to page size *or* the edges themselves.

Trimmed size, the format to which a publication is finally cut, irrespective of the size of the original sheet.

Type specimen, printed example of a complete fount of type in various weights and sizes.

Typeface, a letterform specifically designed to be made up into words and sentences by mechanical means. More than just an alphabet.

Typescale, a ruler marked in point, em and en increments.

Typescript, copy prepared on a typewriter.

Typesetting, text generated in a recognisable typeface.

Typography, the practice of arranging type and the study of type forms. Sometimes used inaccurately in PCs to mean 'typeface'.

U

Ultra, an exaggerated heavy weight of a particular typeface.

Unjustified, text set ranged to the left with the right-hand edge uneven.

Upper case, capital letters.

V

Vectors, (type) lines or arcs plotting the contour of a letterform.

Verso, left-hand page.

W

Watermark, design added to some papers during manufacture. Visible against the light.

White space, blank areas on a page.

Widow, a short line, usually the end of a paragraph, appearing at the top of a page.

Word space, the space left between words in a line.

Wove, an uncoated paper without laid lines.

X

x-height, (type) the height of the lower case letters from the baseline.

Further reading

Bigelow, Charles. 'The Principles of Digital Type', *The Seybold Report* (February 1982)

British Standards Institute, *Draft recommendations for the presentation of tables, graphs and charts* , BSI (London 1977)

Brown, Bruce. *Browns Index to Photocomposition Typography*, Greenwood Publishing (Minehead 1983)

Butcher, Judith. *Copy Editing*, CUP (Cambridge 1975)

Collins, F.Howard. *Authors and Printers' Dictionary*, OUP (Oxford)

Garland, Ken. *Graphics Handbook*, Studio Vista (London 1966)

Hart, Horace. *Rules for Compositors and Readers*, rev edn OUP (Oxford 1967)

Hutt, Allen. *Newspaper Design*, OUP (Oxford 1971)

McLean, Ruari. *Modern Book Design*, Faber & Faber, (London 1958)

Spencer, Herbert. *The Visible Word*, Lund Humphries (London 1969)

Tuft, Edward R. *The Visual Display of Quantitative Information*, Graphics Press (Cheshire, USA)

Tracy, Walter. *Letters of Credit*, Gordon Fraser (London 1986)

Unger, Gerard. *Typography, basic principles and applications*, Oce-Nederland (Venlo, Netherlands 1987)

Williamson Hugh, *Methods of Book Design*, OUP (Oxford 1956)

Index

arrows 55

backing up 30
bibliographical details
 see *imprint pages*
binding 61, 78, 79, 80
bleeds 71
blobs 51, 55
boxes 52, 53, 54
broadsheets see *tabloids*

cannon balls see *blobs*
captions 73
cartoons 68, 69
charts 69, 70
column grids 28, 29-35, 36, 37, 38, 39
colour 77
contents pages 58, 59, 60
cover design 74, 75
cropping illustrations 72
cross references 66

diagrams 68, 69
digitised type see *type*
drawings 68

em 21
emphasis 47-55
en 21
envelope sizes 84

fixed pitch 24
folds 81
footnotes 64, 66
forms 15

graphs 70
grids 28-39
grid sheets 91

half-titles 58, 61
halftones 68, 82, 83
headings, subheadings 11, 42-46, 52, 53, 63, 77
 see also *headlines* and *side headings*
headlines 39
Helvetica 20, 45, 63, 87
horizontal grids 28, 36, 37
hue 77

illustrations 36, 37, 68-73, 74
 list of 61
imprint pages 58, 60
indenting 50, 51, 56, 66
index 35
initial letters 46, 55
instruction manuals 15
introductions 61

journals 38, 76
justified setting 25, 27

laser printers 18, 19, 24, 85
layout 40, 41, 59, 71
 asymmetric layout compared with centred 40, 41
 sketch layouts 86, 90, 92, 93
leading 21
 see also *line spacing*
line counter 28, 90
line illustrations 68
line length 26
line spacing 25, 26, 27
literals 94
lithographic printing see *offset printing*

magazines see *journals*
margins 28, 30, 31, 32
mastheads 76
 see also *headings*
Modern No20 17

negative leading 21
notes
 cut-in 67
 marginal 67
 see also *footnotes*

offset printing 85

paper 82, 83, 84, 85
 paper sizes 84
 varieties of paper 83
photocopiers 77, 85
photographs 68, 71, 72
photomontage 72
pica 20, 21
point system (British American) 20, 21
prelim pages 58-61
printer's marks 94, 96, 97
printing 85
proof-correction marks see *printer's marks*

quotations 56, 57

reproduction, preparing artwork 85
ring binders 30, 80
Rockwell 17
rules 38, 42, 44, 52, 53, 62, 64, 77
running heads 32

sanserif types 17, 54, 63
scaling illustrations 72
section dividers 61, 71
serifed types 17, 54
side headings 30, 31, 46
specifications 94, 95
style manuals 94
subheadings see *headings*

tables 62-65
tabloids 38, 39, 76
Times 17, 19, 20, 45, 63, 88, 89
tints 42, 54, 77
title pages 40, 58, 59
titles see *headings*
tone 77
type, typefaces 16-23, 42, 43, 44, 63, 86
 for captions 73
 design of 16
 digitised 18, 22
 low resolution compared with high resolution 18, 19
 sanserif compared with serif 17, 54, 63
type body 20, 21
type measurement 20, 21
type size 20, 21, 86
type specimens 80
type weights 22, 23
typesetting 24-27
 compared with typewritten text 24

unjustified setting 25, 27

vertical grids see *column grids*

widows 26
word spacing 25, 27